Secrets of the Hand

Soloing Strategies
for Hand Drummers

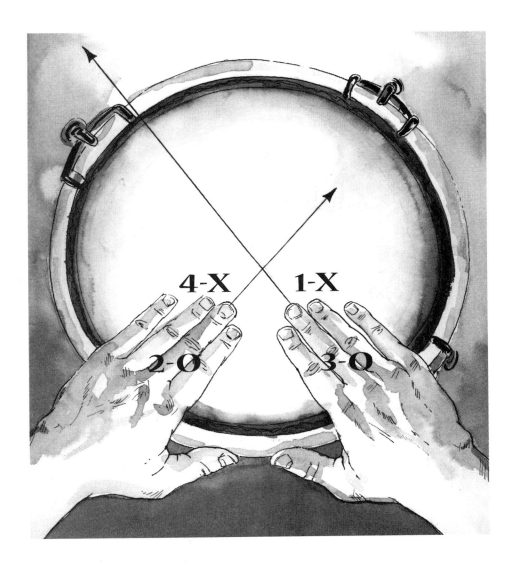

by Alan Dworsky and Betsy Sansby

Cover art by Toni Pawlowsky
Illustrations by Jay Kendell

DANCING HANDS MUSIC

Published by
DANCING HANDS MUSIC
4275 Churchill Circle
Minnetonka, MN, 55345
phone or fax: 952-933-0781
dancinghands.com
email: al@dancinghands.com

Book design and layout by Mighty Media
Cover art by Toni Pawlowsky
Illustrations by Jay Kendell

Printed in the United States of America
with soy ink on recycled, acid-free paper by Banta ISG (Viking Press)

ISBN 0-9638801-6-0

"The hand speaks to the brain as surely as the brain speaks to the hand."

– ROBERTSON DAVIES (from *What's Bred in the Bone*)

Table of Contents

Who this book is for and how it works

This book is for advanced hand drummers who want to play complex solos using simple sequences of hand strokes. Whether you play djembe, conga, or ashiko, the practical hand-pattern strategies explained here will help you get the most out of your hands with the least amount of effort. And whether you want to solo in a traditional African or Afro-Cuban ensemble, in a drum circle, in a band, or in your living room along with your favorite CDs, *Secrets of the Hand* will help you take your playing to the next level.

You don't need great natural hand speed to master the strategies in this book, but you do need a solid understanding of rhythm. You should be comfortable playing in both four and six and have a basic understanding of how cross-rhythms and polyrhythms work. If you don't already have that foundation, one way to get it is from our book *A Rhythmic Vocabulary*. In one sense, *Secrets* is an applied *Rhythmic Vocabulary* for hand drummers. It builds on the patterns and concepts in that book while showing you how to play with maximum ease, consistency, speed, and freedom.

This book is organized into two main sections. Part 1 covers the five basic hand-pattern strategies and Part 2 covers five strategies for creating the illusion of speed. Each new strategy builds on the ones before it. And while you're learning the strategies, you'll also be learning over a hundred patterns that should be a fountain of ideas for you when you solo.

Most of the patterns are based on lead phrases played by djembe and conga drummers in African and Afro-Cuban music. But we're not trying to teach any particular style of drumming. You can use these patterns anywhere with any kind of music as long it has a solid groove. And although we've limited the patterns in this book to those that can be played with just slaps and tones on a single drum, you can certainly use other techniques and additional drums if you like.

The strategies in this book will help you become a more competent soloist. But there's much more to soloing than what can be covered in a book. Great soloists are great storytellers. They know when to speak and when to be silent, when to say little and when to say much, when to let a rhythm simmer and when to bring it to a boil. These skills cannot be taught. They are the result of some mysterious combination of talent, experience, imagination, inspiration, and passion. What can be taught is how to get your head and hands working together more effectively. And that's what this book is all about.

CHAPTER 2

The charts and the count

Here's a sample chart:

PATTERN 4-19

1	+	2	+	3	+	4	+	1	+	2	+	3	+	4	+
O	O		O	O		X		O	O		O	O		X	
	R	L		R	L		R		R	L		R	L		R

Time moves from left to right and each vertical column shows what's happening on a single beat. Each of the three horizontal rows gives you a different kind of information.

The top row tells you how to count a pattern. The symbol "+" stands for "AND." The shaded boxes on the count row indicate the pulse – the underlying metronomic rhythm people feel in their bodies when music is played.

The middle row tells you when and how to hit the drum. If there's a symbol in a box, you hit the drum on that beat with the stroke indicated by the symbol. Here are all the symbols for the different strokes:

Slap	=	**X**
Open tone	=	**O**
ghost note or touch	=	**•**
Flam with two slaps	=	^{x}**X**

Sixteenth notes are indicated by two smaller symbols in a single box. Eighth-note triplets and quarter-note triplets are indicated with curved lines over the stroke symbols:

1	+	2	+	3	+	4	+	1	+	2	+	3	+	4	+
oo O				o	o	o	O			x	x	x	X		
RL R				R	L	R	L			R	L	R	L		

The bottom row on the chart tells you which hand to use. If you're left-handed, you can reverse the hands.

We count patterns in four in cut-time, with two half-notes to a measure. This puts the pulse on beats 1 and 3 in each measure. Each subdivision of the pulse – or beat – is an eighth-note.

We chose to count in cut-time rather than 4/4 for several reasons. We find it's easier to work with two short 8-beat measures than with one long 16-beat measure. We also like the counting system in cut-time better because it gives you a number as a reference point every two beats instead of every four. And we find it easier and more natural to talk about rhythms in cut-time. It's awkward talking about the "ee" of 3 or the "uh" of 4. Finally, tradition played a role in our decision – Afro-Cuban rhythms in four are generally counted in cut-time.

We count patterns in six in 6/8 time, with 6 eighth notes to a measure. The pulse falls on beats 1 and 4 in each measure, and each pulse is divided into three eighth-note beats. Here's a sample chart in six:

PATTERN 4-13

1	2	3	4	5	6	1	2	3	4	5	6
O	O	X		O	O	X		O	O	X	
R	L	R		R	L	R		R	L	R	

We chose to count in 6/8 rather than 12/8 for many of the same reasons we chose to count in cut-time. We find it's easier to work with two short 6-beat measures than with one long 12-beat measure. We like the counting system in 6/8 better because each beat gets its own number. Rhythms in 6/8 are also a lot easier to talk about than rhythms in 12/8. (You already know how we feel about referring to the "uh" of 4.) And finally, tradition again played a role in our decision because Afro-Cuban rhythms in six are generally counted in 6/8 time.

To make the charts as big as possible, we've made them just long enough to show a single repetition of each pattern. But you should think of every chart as being written in a circle. When you get to the end, go back to the beginning and start over without missing a beat.

Think of every chart as being written in a circle. When you get to the end, go back to the beginning and start over without missing a beat.

We haven't put any tempo markings on our charts. Ultimately, the tempo of a rhythm will depend on your playing situation. We recommend that you start slow and gradually increase your speed on each pattern until you can play it as fast as your hands will move. And as soon as you can play a pattern, we recommend that you play it along with a variety of recorded music at different tempos. This will help you understand how the patterns sound in a realistic context. It will also make playing a lot more fun.

The five basic hand-pattern strategies

The easiest way to learn the basic hand-pattern strategies is to stick with the eighth-note grid. That's why all the patterns in Part 1 are made up of eighth notes, with a few quarter-note triplets thrown in. Once you understand how the basic strategies work, you should have no trouble applying them to other grids.

As you work your way through the strategies, remember: they're tools, not rules. If one of them doesn't work for you, don't use it. The important thing is to give each strategy a fair try. That way, even if you ultimately decide to do something different, you'll have a clearer understanding of the choices you're making.

Lead with your strong hand

Let's face it: almost all of us have one hand that's smarter than the other. For about ninety percent of us it's the right hand and for about ten percent it's the left. This trait of handedness probably originated in our prehistoric past, when dinner depended on how good you were at throwing rocks. Stone Age hunters born with the tendency to throw with the same hand every time became good rock throwers twice as fast as those who switched off. This competitive edge allowed them to survive and pass the trait on to their children, who passed it on to us.

But what do you do when you're ready to move from rock-throwing to hand drumming? How do you go from a one-handed skill to a *two*-handed skill where both hands have to perform the same sophisticated movements? Our answer is: if you can't fix it, feature it. Accept your handedness and learn to work with it.

The first strategy for doing this is to lead with your strong hand. There are many applications of this strategy. In this lesson you'll be working with two of them:

1. Lead with your strong hand when you start a pattern.
2. Lead with your strong hand when you change voices.

Accept your handedness and learn to work with it.

Leading with your strong hand when you start a pattern allows you to start strong. Runners in a race take their first step with their strong leg. Why not put your best foot forward when you play?

Leading with your strong hand when you change voices gives your weak hand something to follow. And your weak hand will play a stroke better if it has a chance to watch your strong hand play it first.

Try this experiment. Grab your drum, and with your right hand in your lap, play open tones with your left (we treat the right hand as the strong hand in this book; if you're left-handed, just reverse the hands):

1	+	2	+	3	+	4	+	1	+	2	+	3	+	4	+
O			O					O			O				
L			L					L			L				

How did your left hand do all by itself? Did it feel a little clumsy out there on its own? If it did, it's partly because of another aspect of handedness with roots in our prehistoric past.

Picture a Cro-Magnon man crafting a stone into a spearhead. If he's right-handed, he strikes the stone over and over again with an even harder hammerstone held in his right hand. At the same time, his left hand steadies the stone and responds to each blow of the right hand with a variety of subtle, improvised movements.

By working together in this way on a variety of tasks – pounding, sawing, sewing, carving – over time each hand developed its own area of expertise. The right hand became expert at initiating and repeating specific movements over and over with little variation – the ideal credentials for a future maker of slaps and tones. By contrast, the left hand became expert at anticipating and responding to the actions of the right. Like ballroom dancers, the two hands developed complementary roles. The right learned to lead and the left to follow.

You can see this relationship operating in the Afro-Cuban pattern known as tumbao. In this groove, the right hand takes the lead, making all the slaps and tones. The left hand plays a supporting role, filling in the empty beats with more subtle heel-toe strokes. This natural division of labor between the hands works great on repetitive grooves or support drum parts.

But when you solo, your left hand can no longer play a supporting role. It has to play slaps and tones, and those slaps and tones have to sound exactly like the slaps and tones in your right hand. With enough practice, the left hand can almost meet this challenge. But not quite – at least not for most of us. Even after playing a stroke a million times, the left hand still benefits from that little bit of extra information it gets *in the moment* from watching the right hand go first.

Once it gets that information, your left hand should have no trouble sounding just like the right. You can test out this theory by playing open tones with alternating hands, starting with your right:

PATTERN 1-2

1	+	2	+	3	+	4	+	1	+	2	+	3	+	4	+
O		O		O		O		O		O		O		O	
R		L		R		L		R		L		R		L	

Chances are your left hand did better this time. Through a combination of memory and mimickry, it can sound just like – or almost like – the right.

Even after playing a stroke a million times, the left hand still benefits from that little bit of extra information it gets in the moment from watching the right hand go first.

In the next pattern, your left hand gets to watch your right hand go first every time you change voices. Since the only voices we're concerned with in this book are slaps and tones – the main ingredients of a hand drum solo – changing voices simply means going from slaps to tones or tones to slaps:

PATTERN 1-3

1	+	2	+	3	+	4	+	1	+	2	+	3	+	4	+
X	X	O	O	X	X	O	O	X	X	O	O	X	X	O	O
R	L	R	L	R	L	R	L	R	L	R	L	R	L	R	L

Like butter, right? This pattern is a model of the easiest kind of pattern to play. You lead with your right hand when you start the pattern *and* every time you change voices.

Although leading with your strong hand is the easiest way to play, we don't mean to imply that you *should* always or *can* always follow this strategy. There will be lots of times when you'll need to lead with your weak hand to accomplish a particular musical goal or to play a particular pattern. In the next pattern, for example, you can start with your right hand, but when you switch from slaps to tones you'll have to lead with your left:

PATTERN 1-4

1	2	3	4	5	6	1	2	3	4	5	6
X	X	X	O	O	O	X	X	X	O	O	O
R	L	R	L	R	L	R	L	R	L	R	L

If you replace the tone on 4 with a slap, the pattern gets easier to play. That's because you're back to leading with your strong hand every time you change voices:

PATTERN 1-5

1	2	3	4	5	6	1	2	3	4	5	6
X	X	X	X	O	O	X	X	X	X	O	O
R	L	R	L	R	L	R	L	R	L	R	L

When speed is important, you'll find that "easier" translates into "faster." Try this experiment. Play pattern 1-4 as fast as you can. Then – without stopping – switch to pattern 1-5. You'll notice that you'll be able to speed up. If you switch back, you'll notice you have to slow down to keep each change of voicing clean.

Pattern 1-4 is harder to play not only because you have to lead with your left hand when you change to tones, but also because you're playing strokes in units of *three* – XXX or OOO – with hands that alternate in units of *two* – RL. This adds a layer of complexity that's absent from pattern 1-5. There you're playing strokes in units of two (or multiples of two) – XXXX or OO – with hands that alternate in units of two. The even number of strokes in each voice matches your even number of hands.

Whenever you play a phrase consisting of a continuous series of strokes, you'll automatically get an even number of strokes in each voice as long as you follow both parts of the two-part strategy of leading with your strong hand. Of course if you *end* the phrase with a stroke in your strong hand, the last voicing group will contain an odd number of strokes. But this is no problem, because the last stroke will be followed by a break in your playing:

PATTERN 1-6

1	+	2	+	3	+	4	+	1	+	2	+	3	+	4	+
X	X	O	O	X	X	O	O	O	O	X	X	X			
R	L	R	L	R	L	R	L	R	L	R	L	R			

Sometimes you'll have to choose between leading with your strong hand at the start of a pattern or on changes in voicing. For example, in the next pattern you can do one or the other but not both:

PATTERN 1-7

1	+	2	+	3	+	4	+	1	+	2	+	3	+	4	+
X	O	O	X	X	O	O	X	X							

The advantage of leading with your strong hand at the start is that you get to start – and end – strong:

PATTERN 1-8

1	+	2	+	3	+	4	+	1	+	2	+	3	+	4	+
X	O	O	X	X	O	O	X	X							
R	L	R	L	R	L	R	L	R							

The advantage of leading with your weak hand at the start is that then you get to lead with your strong hand on each change of voicing:

PATTERN 1-9

1	+	2	+	3	+	4	+	1	+	2	+	3	+	4	+
X	O	O	X	X	O	O	X	X							
L	R	L	R	L	R	L	R	L							

We can't tell you which of these hand patterns is better. After you've tried them both, you'll decide for yourself which one you like. This is just the first of many situations in which you'll have to choose between strategies. The best we can hope to do is explain them clearly and show you how they work so you'll understand your options.

Use ghost notes sparingly

Ghost notes are light timekeeping strokes played between the main strokes of a pattern. When they're audible, they add texture and full-ness to your playing. That's a good thing when you're the only drummer in a group and it's your responsibility to lay down a groove.

But when you solo, what's important is not subtle texture, but structure, power, and speed. Except in the most intimate of settings, in order for your solos to be heard you'll need to play at full volume from start to finish. Any subtle texture that ghost notes might add will be lost. Using ghost notes when you solo will only slow you down, tire you out, and trip you up.

When you solo, what's important is not subtle texture, but structure, power, and speed.

To see what we mean, try playing the following pattern as fast and as loud as you can with ghost notes:

PATTERN 2-1

1	+	2	+	3	+	4	+	1	+	2	+	3	+	4	+
X	X	•	•	X	X	•	•	X	X	•	•	X	X	•	•
R	L	R	L	R	L	R	L	R	L	R	L	R	L	R	L

Now try playing the same pattern as fast and as loud as you can *without* ghost notes:

PATTERN 2-2

1	+	2	+	3	+	4	+	1	+	2	+	3	+	4	+
X	X			X	X			X	X			X	X		
R	L			R	L			R	L			R	L		

You probably noticed you could play the pattern faster and louder without the ghost notes. There are several reasons for this. By leaving them out, you cut the number of strokes you make in half. This gives you two empty beats between each pair of slaps to get your hands in the optimal position above the drumhead. From this position, you can bring them down with optimal force.

When you use ghost notes, you don't have that extra time to get in position. And your hands have to switch from minimal intensity to maximum intensity on the fly. The combination of extraneous movements and rushed adjustments hurts your consistency, and cuts your power and speed.

The next pattern illustrates another disadvantage of ghost notes related to the cycle of a figure. A **figure** is a short rhythmic pattern, and the **cycle of a figure** is the number of beats from the start of one repetition of the figure to the start of the next. Whenever you repeat a figure that has a cycle with an *odd* number of beats, if you use ghost notes you'll have to lead with your weak hand on every other repetition.

For example, the figure in the next pattern creates a cross-rhythm with a 3-beat cycle. First play the pattern *with* ghost notes. Make sure to keep a pulse going in your body while you play:

PATTERN 2-3

1	+	2	+	3	+	4	+	1	+	2	+	3	+	4	+
X	X	•	X	X	•	X	X	•	X	X	•	X	X	•	X
R	L	R	L	R	L	R	L	R	L	R	L	R	L	R	L
X															
R															

When you play the pattern *without* ghost notes, you get to lead with your strong hand on every figure. You'll probably notice that you can play the pattern faster and louder without the ghost notes:

PATTERN 2-4

1	+	2	+	3	+	4	+	1	+	2	+	3	+	4	+
X	X		X	X		X	X		X	X		X	X		X
R	L		R	L		R	L		R	L		R	L		R
X															
L															

Here's a similar pattern in six with a 3-beat cycle. First try playing it with ghost notes:

PATTERN 2-5

1	2	3	4	5	6	1	2	3	4	5	6
•	X	X	•	X	X	•	X	X	•	X	X
R	L	R	L	R	L	R	L	R	L	R	L

Once you know the rhythm of the pattern, you should be able to play it faster and louder without ghost notes:

PATTERN 2-6

1	2	3	4	5	6	1	2	3	4	5	6
	X	X		X	X		X	X		X	X
	R	L		R	L		R	L		R	L

When you repeat a figure that has a cycle with an *even* number of beats, using ghost notes isn't as problematic. Although they still slow you down a little, at least they don't reverse your hands on every repetition.

For example, the figures in the next pattern have a 4-beat cycle, just like the figures in pattern 2-1. At slow speeds this pattern is easy to play. But because none of the strokes falls on a pulse, at high speeds it's tricky to play in time. That's when ghost notes can help:

PATTERN 2-7

1	+	2	+	3	+	4	+	1	+	2	+	3	+	4	+
•	•	X	X	•	•	X	X	•	•	X	X	•	•	X	X
R	L	R	L	R	L	R	L	R	L	R	L	R	L	R	L

But the ghost notes in this pattern are like training wheels on a bike. They're helpful at first, but once you know how to ride you can go faster without them:

PATTERN 2-8

1	+	2	+	3	+	4	+	1	+	2	+	3	+	4	+
		X	X			X	X			X	X			X	X
		R	L			R	L			R	L			R	L

Ghost notes can also be useful as a way to get your hands moving in the groove before you launch into a solo or during long breaks between phrases in a solo. But *within* the phrases themselves, we recommend you use ghost notes sparingly.

> ### Ghost notes are like training wheels on a bike. They're helpful at first, but once you know how to ride you can go faster without them.

The best way to minimize your need for ghost notes is to learn to feel the length of the silences between main strokes and figures. And the best way to do that is to learn to vocalize the patterns you want to play.

Drummers around the world have been using this method to learn and memorize rhythms for centuries. In Indian music, for example, there's a highly developed system for vocalizing rhythms. A student may vocalize for a year or more before being allowed to even touch a drum. And in the United States, the Nigerian Babatunde Olatunji has popularized a method of vocalizing in which each syllable tells you the kind of stroke and the hand that plays it.

Most drummers develop their own style of vocalizing. For example, we generally like the sound of "BOP" for slaps and "DOO" for tones. But you can use any syllables you want. And the syllables you use will probably vary from pattern to pattern. The point is: If you can say it – while you tap the pulse – you can play it.

If you can say it – while you tap the pulse – you can play it.

Try using **say-it-and-play-it** now on the following 5-beat cross-rhythm. First get a pulse going in your feet. Then start vocalizing the pattern – without playing it – using any syllables you like. It often helps to wade in slowly, practicing one or two figures at a time before trying to put them all together. It also helps if you can hear each figure as a musical phrase and the whole pattern as a little song:

PATTERN 2-9

1	+	2	+	3	+	4	+	1	+	2	+	3	+	4	+
X	X	X	X		X	X	X	X		X	X	X	X		X
X	X	X		X	X	X	X		X	X	X	X			

Once you can say the pattern, you should have no trouble playing it without ghost notes:

PATTERN 2-9

1	+	2	+	3	+	4	+	1	+	2	+	3	+	4	+
X	X	X	X		X	X	X	X		X	X	X	X		X
R	L	R	L		R	L	R	L		R	L	R	L		R
X	X	X		X	X	X	X		X	X	X	X			
L	R	L		R	L	R	L		R	L	R	L			

Using a one-beat rest between the figures in this cross-rhythm also helps minimize the need for ghost notes. A one-beat rest is the easiest rest to take because it consists of a single unit on the eighth-note grid. Since that grid should be ticking away inside you while you play, all you need to do to take a one-beat rest is stop playing for a single tick of your internal clock.

PLAYING PRINCIPLE

To minimize your need for ghost notes, use a one-beat rest between figures in a cross-rhythm.

Notice how much harder it is to play a 5-beat cross-rhythm with a *two-beat* rest between figures:

PATTERN 2-10

1	+	2	+	3	+	4	+	1	+	2	+	3	+	4	+
X	X	X			X	X	X		X	X	X				X
R	L	R			R	L	R		R	L	R				R
X	X			X	X	X		X	X	X					
L	R			R	L	R		R	L	R					

When figures are parallel – when they have a consistent relationship to the pulse – then taking a longer break between figures isn't a problem, even without ghost notes. But in a cross-rhythm, where the relationship of the figures to the pulse is constantly shifting, if you use anything other than a one-beat rest, you're more likely to get lost.

Alternate hands as much as possible

Alternating hands is a lot like walking. When you walk, you never have to think about which foot comes next. All you have to do is put one foot in front of the other.

When you play with alternating hands, you never have to think about which hand comes next. No matter which hand you start with, left follows right and right follows left, even when there are empty beats between strokes.

Alternating hands is the obvious choice on **continuous figures** – figures *without* empty beats in them. It's also the best choice on most **broken figures** – figures *with* empty beats in them. Here's an example of a broken figure played with alternating hands (the brackets indicate the phrasing of the figure):

PATTERN 3-1

1	+	2	+	3	+	4	+	1	+	2	+	3	+	4	+
[X	X		X	X			O	O]	[X	X		X	X			O	O]
R	L		R	L		R	L	R	L		R	L		R	L

Because you don't have to think about which hand comes next when you use this strategy, it's easy to change the voicing of a figure. In the next chart, we've stacked three different voicings of the figure you just played on top of each other. Notice how easy it is to move from one variation to the next when you use alternating hands, as notated on the bottom row:

1	+	2	+	3	+	4	+	1	+	2	+	3	+	4	+
X	X		X	X		O	O	X	X		X	X		O	O
O	O		X	X		O	O	O	O		X	X		O	O
O	O		O	O		O	O	O	O		O	O		O	O
R	L		R	L		R	L	R	L		R	L		R	L

An alternative strategy that's often used on broken figures is what we call "on-off" style. In **on-off** style, your strong hand plays all the strokes that fall on the on-beats and your weak hand plays all the strokes that fall on the offbeats. In four, the on-beats are the numbered beats and the offbeats are the ANDS. The hand pattern that results is the same as in ghost-note style, except without the ghost notes.

Here's how pattern 3-1 would be played using on-off style. Notice that this time the second pair of slaps in each measure is played LR instead of RL:

1	+	2	+	3	+	4	+	1	+	2	+	3	+	4	+
X	X		X	X		O	O	X	X		X	X		O	O
R	L		L	R		R	L	R	L		L	R		R	L

On-off style works best when you're playing a support drum part over and over without variation. It makes the part easy to remember by turning it into a unique dance with its own distinct shape. The steady flow of information from your hands telling you whether you're playing an on-beat or an offbeat also helps keep you oriented in time.

On-off style makes a support drum part easy to remember by turning it into a unique dance with its own distinct shape.

But on-off style has serious disadvantages when you solo. It slows you down by forcing you to play more than one stroke in a row with the same hand – like the two lefts in a row on the AND of 1 and the AND of 2 in each measure of pattern 3-3. And it makes it hard to change the voicing of a figure because you have to devote so much of your attention to thinking about which hand comes next. You'll see what we mean when you try using on-off style on the same sequence of voicings you played with alternating hands in pattern 3-2:

PATTERN 3-4

1	+	2	+	3	+	4	+	1	+	2	+	3	+	4	+
X	X		X	X		O	O	X	X		X	X		O	O
O	O		X	X		O	O	O	O		X	X		O	O
O	O		O	O		O	O	O	O		O	O		O	O
R	L		L	R		R	L	R	L		L	R		R	L

See what we mean? Alternating hands is obviously the way to go if you want maximum freedom when you solo. And not only does alternating hands make it easy to change the voicing of a figure, it also makes it easy to move smoothly from one figure or pattern to the next.

In the next chart we've combined three different patterns. The first is the pattern you've just been working with, the second is continuous quarter-note triplets (eighth-note triplets if you're counting in 4/4), and the third is the 3-beat cross-rhythm you played in the last lesson. Notice how easy the transitions are when you play all three with alternating hands:

PATTERN 3-5

1	+	2	+	3	+	4	+	1	+	2	+	3	+	4	+
X	X		X	X		O	O	X	X		X	X		O	O
R	L		R	L		R	L	R	L		R	L		R	L
x	x	x	x	x	x	x	x	x	x	x	x				
R	L	R	L	R	L	R	L	R	L	R	L				
X	X		X	X		X	X		X	X		X	X		X
R	L		R	L		R	L		R	L		R	L		R
X															
L															

You can even use alternating hands on a series of offbeats. Try it now on the following two-measure broken figure, which ends with a series of offbeats. Notice we lead with the left hand at the start of the pattern so we can lead with the right on the two changes in voicing that follow:

PATTERN 3-6

1	+	2	+	3	+	4	+	1	+	2	+	3	+	4	+
	X	O	O	X	X		X		X		X		X		X
	L	R	L	R	L		R		L		R		L		R

In the next chart, we've created a longer pattern, the kind you might want to use in a solo. It starts with the figure you just played repeated three times and ends with a few extra strokes that allow you to land on a pulse:

1	+	2	+	3	+	4	+	1	+	2	+	3	+	4	+
X	O	O	X	X			X		X		X		X		X
L	R	L	R	L			R		L		R		L		R
X	O	O	X	X			X		X		X		X		X
L	R	L	R	L			R		L		R		L		R
X	O	O	X	X			X		X		X		X		X
L	R	L	R	L			R		L		R		L		R
X		X	X												
L		R	L												

As you can tell from playing this pattern, alternating hands works fine on a short series of offbeats. But the longer a series of offbeats gets, the harder it is to play with alternating hands. That's because after a while the on-beats start to tug at your hands like magnets. The longer and faster you play, the stronger the force becomes.

To see what we mean, try playing pure offbeats with alternating hands now. Play along with some external reference – a metronome, a time-line, a recorded song, whatever you like – and see how long you can hang on:

1	+	2	+	3	+	4	+	1	+	2	+	3	+	4	+
	X		X		X		X		X		X		X		X
	R		L		R		L		R		L		R		L

How did you do? Pretty hard, isn't it? Is your neck sore from nodding on every empty beat? Playing ghost notes with your head is a lot of work.

Now watch what happens when you try the same thing again using just your right hand:

PATTERN 3-9

1	+	2	+	3	+	4	+	1	+	2	+	3	+	4	+
	X		X		X		X		X		X		X		X
	R		R		R		R		R		R		R		R

Surprisingly easy, wasn't it? It's just as easy with your left hand:

PATTERN 3-10

1	+	2	+	3	+	4	+	1	+	2	+	3	+	4	+
X		X		X		X		X		X		X		X	
L		L		L		L		L		L		L		L	

The reason this pattern is easier to play with one hand than with two is that both hands have spent countless hours alternating on the eighth-note grid, each hand playing every other beat. If you're right-handed, your left hand has probably spent most of its time playing offbeats, so this pattern isn't really all that new. The only difference is that the right hand isn't playing along:

1	+	2	+	3	+	4	+	1	+	2	+	3	+	4	+
X	X	X	X	X	X	X	X	X	X	X	X	X	X	X	X
R	L	R	L	R	L	R	L	R	L	R	L	R	L	R	L

And even though your right hand has probably spent most of its time playing on-beats, it should have little trouble switching to offbeats because it has the same "every-other-beat" distance securely stored in its muscle memory. All it needs to do is shift that interval from the on-beats to the offbeats:

1	+	2	+	3	+	4	+	1	+	2	+	3	+	4	+
X	**X**	X	**X**	X	**X**	X	**X**	X	**X**	X	**X**	X	**X**	X	**X**
L	**R**	L	**R**	L	**R**	L	**R**	L	**R**	L	**R**	L	**R**	L	**R**

PLAYING PRINCIPLE

Play a long series of offbeats with one hand.

So if you want to play a long series of offbeats, you'll probably want to deviate from an alternating hands strategy and play them with just one hand. It's an easy way to impress your friends. And once you get good at it, you can create a dramatic effect by doing something flashy with your other hand. For example, Madou Dembele, a master djembe player from Mali, entertained an audience at the Jembe Institute in North Carolina by pretending to answer his cell phone while playing this lick. Combing your hair or karate-chopping the air with your free hand also looks cool.

Here's the equivalent pattern in six. We can't technically call it the offbeats in six because the stroke on 4 coincides with a pulse. So we'll just call it the even-numbered beats. Playing this series with alternating hands is easier than playing the offbeats in four. That's because you're never left hanging for too long. In the middle of each measure you get to touch down on a pulse:

PATTERN 3-11

1	2	3	4	5	6	1	2	3	4	5	6
	X		X		X		X		X		X
	R		L		R		L		R		L

But playing the even-numbered beats with one hand is even easier than playing them with two:

PATTERN 3-12

1	2	3	4	5	6	1	2	3	4	5	6
	X		X		X		X		X		X
	R		R		R		R		R		R

So if you're playing a long series of offbeats in four or the even-numbered beats in six, it's easiest to use one hand. Otherwise, alternate hands as much as possible.

Play repeating figures the same way every time

Alternating hands works great on most figures. That's why in the last lesson we recommended you do it as much as possible. But when you're working with a repeating figure, it's usually best to play the figure the same way every time – even if that means you have to break the flow of alternating hands *between* figures.

By **repeating figure**, we mean a figure that stays exactly the same on every repetition, keeping the same structure *and the same voicing*. And when we recommend that you play a repeating figure the same way every time, we mean you should use *the same hand pattern* on every repetition, starting with the same hand every time.

The strategy of playing repeating figures the same way every time is only necessary for **odd figures** – figures with an odd number of strokes. **Even figures** – figures with an even number of strokes – don't require a new strategy. As long as you alternate hands on an even figure itself, you'll automatically end up playing it the same way every time.

Here's an example of a repeating even figure with four strokes. It's a variation of the 5-beat cross-rhythm you played in Lesson 2. Notice that there's no need to break the flow of alternating hands between figures:

PATTERN 4-1

1	+	2	+	3	+	4	+	1	+	2	+	3	+	4	+
X	X	O	O		X	X	O	O		X	X	O	O		X
R	L	R	L		R	L	R	L		R	L	R	L		R
X	O	O		X	X	O	O		X	X	O	O			
L	R	L		R	L	R	L		R	L	R	L			

Odd figures are different. To play an odd figure the same way every time, you have to break the flow of alternating hands when you move from one repetition to the next. This means you have to play two strokes in a row with the same hand – at the end of one repetition and at the beginning of the next.

That's what you'll do with the seven-stroke figure in the next chart. You still alternate hands *within* each figure, but when you move from one repetition to the next you have to play two rights in a row:

PATTERN 4-2

1	+	2	+	3	+	4	+	1	+	2	+	3	+	4	+
	O	O	O	O	X	X	X		O	O	O	O	X	X	X
	R	L	R	L	R	L	R		R	L	R	L	R	L	R

If you don't break the flow of alternating hands, you have to reverse the hand pattern on every repetition. This forces you to lead with your weak hand at the start of the figure and on the change of voicing within the figure:

PATTERN 4-3

1	+	2	+	3	+	4	+	1	+	2	+	3	+	4	+
	O	O	O	O	X	X	X		O	O	O	O	X	X	X
	R	L	R	L	R	L	R		L	R	L	R	L	R	L

As you can see, playing a repeating odd figure the same way every time is easier. You get to pick one hand pattern and stick with it. The result is that you get the most consistent sound with the least amount of thought and effort.

This strategy also makes your practicing more efficient. When you only have to learn how to play a figure one way, you can learn twice as many figures in the same amount of time. Although there will be exceptions, it's inefficient to *routinely* learn to start figures with either hand. Why learn to play fifty figures in two ways when you can learn to play a hundred figures instead?

An underlined
symbol indicates
you should start
playing the pattern
there.

Let's try the strategy with another odd figure. This one is in six and it has five strokes. We've underlined the X on 3 in the first measure to indicate you should start playing there. Notice that again you play two rights in a row when you move from one repetition to the next:

PATTERN 4-4

1	2	3	4	5	6	1	2	3	4	5	6
X		X	X	O	O	X		X	X	O	O
R		R	L	R	L	R		R	L	R	L

The next odd figure also has five strokes. But this one starts with the left hand. Notice that this time when you move from one repetition of the figure to the next, you have to play two *lefts* in a row:

PATTERN 4-5

1	+	2	+	3	+	4	+	1	+	2	+	3	+	4	+
X	O	O	X	X		X	O	O	X	X		X	O	O	X
L	R	L	R	L		L	R	L	R	L		L	R	L	R
X															
L															

That brings us to three-stroke figures, the shortest odd figures there are. In general, it's still easiest to play them the same way every time. But because three-stroke figures are so short, the choice between strategies is a closer call than it is with longer odd figures. That's because the shorter the repeating figure, the more often you have to break the flow of alternating hands.

For example, to play the three-stroke figures in the next pattern the same way every time, you have to break the flow every fourth beat. In addition, your right hand has to play twice as many strokes as your left. But you'll find it's still the easiest way to play these figures and the best way to get the most consistent sound:

PATTERN 4-6

1	+	2	+	3	+	4	+	1	+	2	+	3	+	4	+
X		X	X	X		X	X	X		X	X	X		X	X
R		R	L	R		R	L	R		R	L	R		R	L

If you prefer to distribute the work evenly between your hands, your other choice is to play this pattern using **pure alternating hands**. This simply means continuing the flow of alternating hands from figure to figure even though it reverses the hand pattern on every repetition:

PATTERN 4-7

1	+	2	+	3	+	4	+	1	+	2	+	3	+	4	+
X		X	X	X		X	X	X		X	X	X		X	X
R		L	R	L		R	L	R		L	R	L		R	L

Using pure alternating hands evens out the workload and makes it easy to move smoothly from this pattern to other patterns. But playing the figures the same way every time takes less practice and gives you the most consistent sound. Which of these hand-pattern strategies you decide to use will depend on many factors, including how long you're playing the pattern, how fast, how even your hands are in ability, what the voicing is, and where you're headed.

You can see which strategy you like best by playing the next pattern both ways. As you repeat it over and over, you'll be switching back and forth between the pattern you just played and quarter-note triplets. Try it first playing the three-stroke figures the same way every time:

1	+	2	+	3	+	4	+	1	+	2	+	3	+	4	+
X		X	X	X		X	X	X		X	X	X		X	X
R		R	L	R		R	L	R		R	L	R		R	L
X⌢		X	X	X⌢		X	X	X⌢		X	X	X⌢		X	X
R		L	R	L		R	L	R		L	R	L		R	L

Now play the same pattern using pure alternating hands:

PATTERN 4-9

1	+	2	+	3	+	4	+	1	+	2	+	3	+	4	+
X		X	X	X		X	X	X		X	X	X		X	X
R		L	R	L		R	L	R		L	R	L		R	L
X⌢		X	X	X⌢		X	X	X⌢		X	X	X⌢		X	X
R		L	R	L		R	L	R		L	R	L		R	L

Which did you like better? Whichever one it was, make a mental note for next time.

Here's a fun trick you can do with voicing when you play the three-stroke figures with pure alternating hands. Play just slaps with one hand and just tones with the other, and listen to what happens: each hand ends up playing the one-bar clave. The right hand's version starts on 1, while the left hand's version is shifted over to start on 3. When you're first learning this pattern, it's easier if you just forget about the claves and focus on the figures. The clave patterns will emerge on their own:

PATTERN 4-10

1	+	2	+	3	+	4	+	1	+	2	+	3	+	4	+
X		O	X	O		X	O	X		O	X	O		X	O
R		L	R	L		R	L	R		L	R	L		R	L

One-bar
clave

Shifted
one-bar clave

You can do the same thing in reverse by putting tones in the right hand and slaps in the left:

PATTERN 4-11

1	+	2	+	3	+	4	+	1	+	2	+	3	+	4	+
O		X	O	X		O	X	O		X	O	X		O	X
R		L	R	L		R	L	R		L	R	L		R	L

When you take our original three-stroke figures and play them in six, you get what's called an "abakwa" pattern in Afro-Cuban rhythms. The abakwa pattern creates the polyrhythm of 3 over 4. The three-stroke figures imply a 3-pulse over an underlying 4-pulse. In this context, the three-note figures are much easier if you play them the same way every time:

PATTERN 4-12

1	2	3	4	5	6	1	2	3	4	5	6
X	X	X		X	X	X		X	X	X	
R	L	R		R	L	R		R	L	R	

The reason using pure alternating hands in this context is so much harder is that it takes a full four measures to complete the hand pattern:

PATTERN 4-13

1	2	3	4	5	6	1	2	3	4	5	6
X	X	X		X	X	X		X	X	X	
R	L	R		L	R	L		R	L	R	
X	X	X		X	X	X		X	X	X	
L	R	L		R	L	R		L	R	L	

When you use more than one voice in the figures, you'll need to play them the same way every time to get the most consistent sound:

PATTERN 4-14

1	2	3	4	5	6	1	2	3	4	5	6
O	O	X		O	O	X		O	O	X	
R	L	R		R	L	R		R	L	R	

This is about the place where we'd normally end a lesson. But because there's so much to say about this strategy, we're going to push on. Of course that doesn't mean you can't take a break. As a matter of fact, we recommend you put the book down now (if you haven't already) and get yourself a sandwich. Relax for a while. That's what we're going to do. Then we can all come back when we're refreshed.

Okay, everybody ready to move on? Before the break we were talking about repeating continuous figures, figures without empty beats in them. Now we're going to talk about broken figures – figures with empty beats within them. Just like continuous figures, repeating broken figures are usually best played the same way every time.

We'll start with the 6/8 bell pattern, a broken odd figure with seven strokes. One traditional phrasing of this pattern starts on 3 in the first measure, and that's where you'll start playing. To play the figure the same way every time, you'll break the flow of alternating hands at the end of the phrase, after the tone on 1 in the first measure. That means you'll play two rights in a row on 1 and 3 in the first measure:

PATTERN 4-15

1	2	3	4	5	6	1	2	3	4	5	6
O		X̲		X	X		X		O		O
R		R		L	R		L		R		L

Putting the break in the flow of alternating hands in a different place can inspire different voicings. For example, putting the break between 3 and 5 in the first measure suggests the following voicings:

PATTERN 4-16

1	2	3	4	5	6	1	2	3	4	5	6
O		O		X̲	X		X		X		O
L		R		R	L		R		L		R

PATTERN 4-17

1	2	3	4	5	6	1	2	3	4	5	6
O		O		X̲	X		O		O		O
L		R		R	L		R		L		R

Breaking the flow of alternating hands in a different place can inspire different voicings.

1	2	3	4	5	6	1	2	3	4	5	6
O		X		O	O		X		X		O
L		R		R	L		R		L		R

Here's another common broken figure. This one has five strokes. It's the reverse image of the one-bar clave. That means it's created by putting strokes on all the empty beats in the one-bar clave pattern and then leaving out the one-bar clave itself. The figure fits neatly within a measure of four, so the break in the flow of alternating hands comes between measures:

1	+	2	+	3	+	4	+	1	+	2	+	3	+	4	+
	O	O			O	O		X			O	O			O	O		X
	R	L			R	L		R			R	L			R	L		R

Now try adding a series of offbeats to the figure. This creates a single two-measure figure with 9 strokes. We've notated alternating hands for the offbeats but you can play them with one hand if you want:

1	+	2	+	3	+	4	+	1	+	2	+	3	+	4	+
	O	O			O	O		X		X		X		X		X
	R	L			R	L		R		L		R		L		R

You can create a longer phrase by combining the last two patterns:

PATTERN 4-21

1	+	2	+	3	+	4	+	1	+	2	+	3	+	4	+
	O	O		O	O		X		O	O		O	O		X
	R	L		R	L		R		R	L		R	L		R
	O	O		O	O		X	X		X		X		X	
	R	L		R	L		R	L		R		L		R	

In the next pattern, you're going to play a *three*-stroke broken figure the same way every time. But you're going to play it RRL so you can lead with your strong hand on every change of voicing. The figures create a 5-beat cross-rhythm in four:

PATTERN 4-22

1	+	2	+	3	+	4	+	1	+	2	+	3	+	4	+
			O	O	X			O	O	X			O	O	X
			R	L	R			R	L	R			R	L	R
X															
R															

Still with us? Good. There's just one important exception to the strategy of playing a broken odd figure the same way every time: when you use *a single voice*, it's easier to use pure alternating hands. That's because without the varied terrain created by two voices, there aren't any landmarks to tell you when to break the flow of alternating hands. With *pure* alternating hands, all you have to do is keep putting one hand in front of the other. As long as you know the rhythm, your hands will take care of themselves. And you won't have to worry about leading with your weak hand on changes in voicing because … there are no changes in voicing.

Use pure
alternating hands
when you play
a repeating
broken figure in
a single voice.

Try this strategy now on the 6/8 bell pattern, a rhythm you already know. Play the pattern with pure alternating hands using just tones. Even though it takes four measures before you start the figure again with your right hand, if you concentrate on the rhythm, your hands will take care of themselves:

PATTERN 4-23

1	2	3	4	5	6	1	2	3	4	5	6
O		O		O	O		O		O		O
R		L		R	L		R		L		R
O		O		O	O		O		O		O
L		R		L	R		L		R		L

Now try playing pattern 4-19 with pure alternating hands using just tones. Again, once you know the rhythm, your hands will take care of themselves:

PATTERN 4-24

1	+	2	+	3	+	4	+	1	+	2	+	3	+	4	+
O	O			O	O		O	O	O			O	O		O
R	L			R	L		R	L	R			L	R		L

And finally, try playing pattern 4-22 with pure alternating hands using just tones. Just make sure you can say it before you try to play it:

PATTERN 4-25

1	+	2	+	3	+	4	+	1	+	2	+	3	+	4	+
	O		O	O		O		O	O		O		O	O	
	R		L	R		L		R	L		R		L	R	
O															
L															

Since this lesson was so long, let's to take a minute to review what we've said about repeating figures. In general, we recommended that you break the flow of alternating hands in order to play a figure the same way every time.

We focused on odd figures because breaking the flow isn't an issue with even figures. With odd figures – whether continuous or broken – playing a figure the same way every time is generally easier and gets you the most consistent sound. This is true even on three-stroke figures, the shortest odd figures there are, although it's a close call.

The main exception occurs when you're playing a broken odd figure using only one voice. Then – as long as you know the rhythm – it's easier to use pure alternating hands and reverse the hand pattern on every repetition.

Camouflage with alternating pairs

Camouflaging is the use of voicing to disguise the structure of a pattern. It's a simple technique for creating the illusion of complexity.

The easiest voicing pattern to use for camouflaging is **alternating pairs** of slaps and tones: XXOO or OOXX. You can play them continuously or with empty beats between strokes. Because playing alternating pairs takes almost no thought, your brain is free to focus on rhythm.

Let's start in six. When you play alternating pairs with the voicing pattern XXOO they imply a 3-pulse that camouflages the underlying 4-pulse. In order to feel the polyrhythm, be sure to tap your foot on the 4-pulse while you play :

PATTERN 5-1

1	2	3	4	5	6	1	2	3	4	5	6
X	X	O	O	X	X	O	O	X	X	O	O
R	L	R	L	R	L	R	L	R	L	R	L

3-Pulse

If you're finding it hard to feel the 4-pulse, practice counting each pulse out loud while you play: 1, 2, 3, 4. Just make sure you don't accent the 4-pulse in your hands or you'll give away the secret:

PATTERN 5-1

1			2			3			4		
X	X	O	O	X	X	O	O	X	X	O	O
R	L	R	L	R	L	R	L	R	L	R	L

While you did this exercise, you may have noticed where the 4-pulse fell in your hands. The first pulse falls on a slap in your right hand, the second on a tone in your left, the third on a tone in your right, and the fourth on a slap in your left:

PATTERN 5-1

1	2	3	4	5	6	1	2	3	4	5	6
X	X	O	O	X	X	O	O	X	X	O	O
R	L	R	L	R	L	R	L	R	L	R	L

Here's how this sequence looks as it moves from hand to hand on the drumhead:

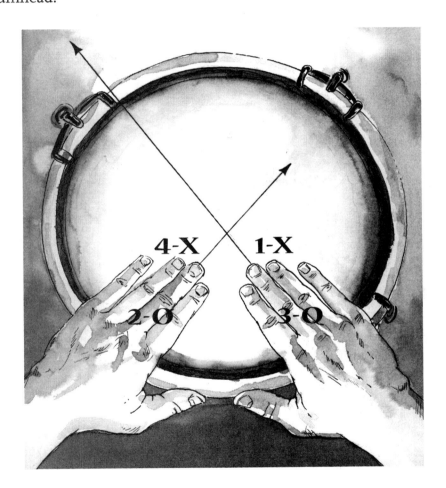

You can watch this sequence while you play to help you keep track of the 4-pulse. And if you're ever up in the middle of the night with nothing else to do, you can visualize the sequence in your head. It's great practice, and it usually puts you right back to sleep. Even if it doesn't, it beats lying there worrying about whether you remembered to turn off the oven.

Now play alternating pairs starting with tones:

PATTERN 5-2

1	2	3	4	5	6	1	2	3	4	5	6
O	O	X	X	O	O	X	X	O	O	X	X
R	L	R	L	R	L	R	L	R	L	R	L

When you start with tones, the 4-pulse moves from hand to hand in the following order:

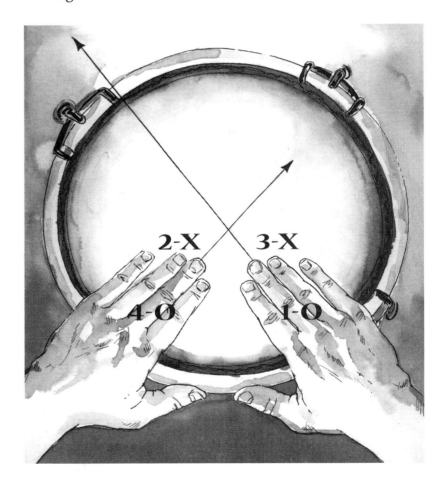

Once you're able to feel the 4-pulse in six while playing alternating pairs, you're ready to camouflage quarter-note triplets in four. While you play, you're going to need to be listening to something in four to establish the underlying eighth-note grid. So get up now and pop something you like into your CD player. It'll only take a second, and this exercise only makes sense if you're playing along with music.

Got the music playing? Great. Start by playing triplets with just slaps to warm up:

PATTERN 5-3

1	+	2	+	3	+	4	+	1	+	2	+	3	+	4	+
x	x	x	x	x	x	x	x	x	x	x	x
R	L	R	L	R	L	R	L	R	L	R	L

When you're comfortable playing the triplets, you're ready to try camouflaging them. You may want to start with just slaps to get your hands moving at the right speed before you transition into alternating pairs:

PATTERN 5-4

1	+	2	+	3	+	4	+	1	+	2	+	3	+	4	+
x	x	o	o	x	x	o	o	x	x	o	o
R	L	R	L	R	L	R	L	R	L	R	L

It's critical that you feel the 4-pulse at all times while you play this pattern. If you start feeling the 3-pulse implied by the alternating pairs, you're lost. And once you're lost, the only way back is to stop playing and listen until you find the 4-pulse again, something you don't want to get caught doing in public.

In the next pattern, you're going to move from three-stroke figures to triplets and then to camouflaged triplets. The hand pattern on the chart for the three-stroke figures is pure alternating hands, but you can play the figures the same way every time if you like:

PATTERN 5-5

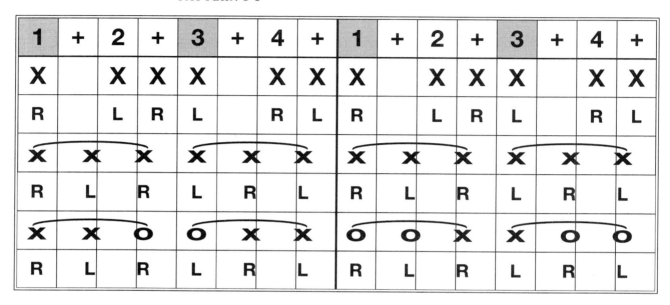

Next you're going to work with a pattern made up of two-stroke figures that create a 3-beat cross-rhythm in four. You played these figures in earlier lessons starting on ONE. Here the figures start on the beat after ONE and end on ONE two cycles later. Before you try camouflaging them with alternating pairs, try playing them with just slaps. Play each figure RL:

PATTERN 5-6

1	+	2	+	3	+	4	+	1	+	2	+	3	+	4	+
	X	X		X	X		X	X		X	X		X	X	
X	X		X	X		X	X		X	X		X	X		X
X															

When you play these two-stroke figures with alternating pairs of slaps and tones, they turn into four-stroke figures that create a 6-beat cross-rhythm. This is a pretty minor "camouflage" – kind of like taping on a paper moustache – but it does change your perception of the structure of the pattern:

PATTERN 5-7

1	+	2	+	3	+	4	+	1	+	2	+	3	+	4	+
	X	X		O	O			X	X		O	O		X	X
O	O		X	X		O	O		X	X		O	O		X
X															

In the next pattern, we start with two short phrases that pique the listener's interest and announce the theme of the more complex cross-rhythm to come. Within that cross-rhythm, we've delayed the start of the alternating pairs for a full cycle. So when the alternating pairs take over, the new structure they imply comes as a surprise:

PATTERN 5-8

1	+	2	+	3	+	4	+	1	+	2	+	3	+	4	+
	X	X		X	X										
	X	X		X	X										
	X	X		X	X			X	X		X	X		X	X
O	O		X	X		O	O		X	X		O	O		X
X															

The next pattern has the same structure as the pattern you just played, but this time the alternating pairs have been shifted. Each member of each pair has been separated from its partner by an empty beat. If the previous camouflage was a paper moustache, this is deep cover:

PATTERN 5-9

1	+	2	+	3	+	4	+	1	+	2	+	3	+	4	+
	X	X		X	X										
	X	X		X	X										
	X	X		X	X				X	X		X	X		
X	O		O	X		X	O		O	X		X	O		O
X															

Now listen to what happens when you continue playing the two-stroke figures with shifted alternating pairs for an additional cycle and a half:

PATTERN 5-10

1	+	2	+	3	+	4	+	1	+	2	+	3	+	4	+
	X	X		X	X										
	X	X		X	X										
	X	X		X	X				X	X		X	X		
X	O		O	X		X	O		O	X		X	O		O
X		X	O		O	X		X	O		O	X		X	O
	O	X		X	O		O	X							

You probably noticed at some point during the second cycle of shifted alternating pairs that the pattern got reconfigured in your mind. Instead of hearing the repeating figure as XOOX, you started hearing it as XXOO:

1	+	2	+	3	+	4	+	1	+	2	+	3	+	4	+
X	O		O	X		X	O		O	X		X	O		O

Original pattern   Reconfigured pattern

This reconfiguration is the result of the ear's tendency to group strokes in the same voice together. We hear the two slaps as connected and the two tones as connected, even though each pair is split down the middle by an empty beat.

But this tendency to group strokes in the same voice together doesn't kick in right away. It takes several repetitions of the figures before the reconfiguration occurs. Exactly how many repetitions will depend on many factors, including the listener's level of experience and what else is being played around your solo. The main point is that this reconfiguration is likely to change the listener's perception of the pulse and create a disorienting effect.

When you solo, it's your job to know the effect you're having on your listeners. In this case, that means knowing approximately when the disorienting effect will occur. That way you can make a conscious decision whether to cross that line or stop short of it.

Our intention with the original pattern – pattern 5-9 – was to stop just before crossing the line. We wanted to create some tension and rhythmic ambiguity, but we didn't want to throw the listener for a loop. It's one thing to give your dance partner a single spin. It's another to wind them up and send them reeling across the floor. That's what's likely to happen with a pattern like pattern 5-10. So you probably want to save that move for experienced dance partners.

If you want to lead with your strong hand on the changes in voicing when you play shifted alternating pairs, you can. All you have to do is start the pattern with your left hand. Then you'll be set to lead with your right on all the changes in voicing that follow. Notice that this means you'll be playing each two-stroke figure LR:

PLAYING PRINCIPLE

When you solo, know the effect you're having on your listeners.

1	+	2	+	3	+	4	+	1	+	2	+	3	+	4	+
X	O		O	X		X	O		O	X		X	O		O
L	R		L	R		L	R		L	R		L	R		L
X															
R															

Here's a longer phrase that starts with shifted alternating pairs. Try playing the two-stroke figures RL and LR to see which feels easier and more natural to you:

PATTERN 5-12

1	+	2	+	3	+	4	+	1	+	2	+	3	+	4	+
	O	X		X	O		O	X		X	O		O	X	
	O	X		X	O		O	X		X	O		O	X	
	O	X		X	O		O	X		X	O		O	X	
X	O		O	X		X	O		O	X		X	O		O
X															

The next pattern uses alternating pairs in six. In the first two cycles there's no camouflaging going on because the two-stroke figures fit evenly within each pulse. But when you shift the alternating pairs, the camouflage kicks in. Play each two-stroke figure RL. And notice that you play three slaps in a row when the pattern repeats – one at the end and two at the beginning:

PATTERN 5-13

1	2	3	4	5	6	1	2	3	4	5	6
	X	X		O	O		X	X		O	O
	X	X		O	O		X	X		O	O
	X	O		O	X		X	O		O	X
	X	O		O	X		X	O		O	X

You can create the illusion that time is slowing down by switching from two-stroke figures to camouflaging the even-numbered beats. In the first half of the next pattern it feels like you're moving through air; in the second half, like you're moving through water. You should be able to play the whole pattern with alternating hands. If you feel yourself getting seasick on the even-numbered beats, remember to check your pulse on 4. If that doesn't help, go back to say-it-and-play-it until you can hear the song:

PATTERN 5-14

1	2	3	4	5	6	1	2	3	4	5	6
	X	X		O	O		X	X		O	O
	X	X		O	O		X	X		O	O
	X		X		O	O		X		X	
	O		O		X	X		O		O	

Congratulations! You've just completed the five basic hand pattern strategies. Now it's time to pick up the pace.

Five strategies for creating the illusion of speed

In Part 2, you'll continue to apply the five basic hand-pattern strategies while adding faster strokes. But don't worry. We aren't going to ask you to play long blasts of thirty-second notes at superhuman speed. And we're not going to get into double-strokes or paradiddles – techniques that are hard to master and aren't very versatile. Instead, you're going to learn how to use a minimum number of faster strokes to create the maximum illusion of speed.

Create a ripple effect with two sixteenth notes or an eighth-note triplet

To create the maximum illusion of speed with the minimum amount of effort, you need to take advantage of what we call **the ripple effect**. Here's how it works. Whenever faster strokes are immediately followed by slower strokes, it takes the ear a while to adjust. And while it's adjusting, the impression of speed lingers, rippling forward into the slower strokes until the ear can sort things out. This is one reason drummers usually put faster strokes at the start of a figure rather than at the end. If you start with slower strokes and end with faster strokes, you cut off the ripple effect before it has a chance to start.

And here's good news for all of us who aren't genetically endowed with lightning-fast hands: All it takes to generate the ripple effect is a single pair of sixteenth notes or an eighth-note triplet. (If you're thinking in 4/4, this translates to a single pair of thirty-second notes or a sixteenth-note triplet.) We'll show you how this works using the following figures consisting of straight eighth notes:

PATTERN 6-1

1	+	2	+	3	+	4	+	1	+	2	+	3	+	4	+
O	O	O	O	O	O			O	O	O	O	O	O		
R	L	R	L	R	L			R	L	R	L	R	L		

Now add a single pair of sixteenth notes at the start of each figure. Play the pattern at high speed and listen for the ripple effect. Notice we've underlined the first of the two sixteenth notes on the AND of 4 in the second measure to indicate you should start playing there:

PATTERN 6-2

1	+	2	+	3	+	4	+	1	+	2	+	3	+	4	+
O	O	O	O	O	O		oo	O	O	O	O	O	O		<u>oo</u>
R	L	R	L	R	L		RL	R	L	R	L	R	L		RL

PLAYING PRINCIPLE

The faster you play, the harder it is for the ear to distinguish a change in speed and the further the ripple effect extends.

See what we mean? Could your ear distinguish exactly when the sixteenth notes ended and the eighth notes began? Not unless you played the figures really slowly. The faster you play, the harder it is for the ear to distinguish a change in speed and the further the ripple effect extends.

Usually the ripple effect will die out on its own after a few eighth notes. But you can hasten its demise by changing voices. In the next pattern, you'll switch from tones to slaps immediately after playing the sixteenth notes. You'll still get a little ripple, but it won't extend very far:

PATTERN 6-3

1	+	2	+	3	+	4	+	1	+	2	+	3	+	4	+
X	X	X	X	X	X		oo	X	X	X	X	X	X		<u>oo</u>
R	L	R	L	R	L		RL	R	L	R	L	R	L		RL

PLAYING PRINCIPLE

Downshift before changing voices to get the most mileage out of the ripple effect.

To get the most mileage out of the ripple effect, we recommend you downshift before changing voices. **Downshifting** simply means moving from faster to slower strokes while staying in the same voice. In addition to extending the ripple effect, this makes figures easier to play because you don't have to change speeds *and* voices at the same time.

In the next pattern you're going to play the same figures you just played, only this time you'll downshift before changing voices. This allows you to squeeze all the ripple out of the tones before moving on to the slaps:

1	+	2	+	3	+	4	+	1	+	2	+	3	+	4	+
O	O	O	O	X	X		oo	O	O	O	O	X	X		<u>oo</u>
R	L	R	L	R	L		RL	R	L	R	L	R	L		RL

You can also generate a ripple effect with a single eighth-note triplet, but it takes a little more strategizing. In four, it's easiest to start a triplet on an on-beat – the numbered beats on our charts. When you do that, the note *following* the triplet will also fall on an on-beat. This gives you solid reference points at both the beginning and the end of the triplet.

It's harder to start a triplet on an offbeat – the ANDs on our charts in four. If you do, the note following the triplet also falls on an offbeat. This means you don't have a solid reference point at either the beginning or the end of the triplet. To see what we mean, try starting the figures you just played with eighth-note triplets instead of sixteenth notes:

PATTERN 6-5

1	+	2	+	3	+	4	+	1	+	2	+	3	+	4	+
o o	O	O	O	X	X		o o o	O	O	O	X	X		o o
R	L	R	L	R	L		R	R	L	R	L	R	L		R

Hard, right? It gets easier if you shift the figures back a beat so each triplet starts on an on-beat instead:

PATTERN 6-6

1	+	2	+	3	+	4	+	1	+	2	+	3	+	4	+
O	O	O	X	X		o o o	O	O	O	X	X			<u>o</u> o o	
L	R	L	R	L		R	R	L	R	L	R	L			R	R

Once you shift the figures so they start on on-beats, starting with triplets is even easier than starting with sixteenth notes. With the triplets you get to re-enter the eighth-note grid on 1 – a nice solid spot to aim for. With a pair of sixteenth notes, you have to re-enter on the AND of 4 – a more difficult target to hit:

PATTERN 6-7

1	+	2	+	3	+	4	+	1	+	2	+	3	+	4	+
O	O	O	X	X		oo	O	O	O	O	X	X		oo	O
L	R	L	R	L		RL	R	L	R	L	R	L		RL	R

PLAYING
PRINCIPLE

Your maximum
overall playing
speed will always be
limited by how fast
you can play the
fastest notes in a
pattern.

Another advantage to starting these figures with eighth-note triplets is that this allows you to increase your overall speed on the pattern. That's because your overall speed will always be limited by how fast you can play the fastest notes in a pattern. It's true that there are three notes in the triplet as opposed to two sixteenth notes. But the notes of the triplet are only one and a half times as fast as the eighth notes and you get to spread them evenly across a span of *two* beats. The sixteenth notes are *twice* as fast as the eighth notes and you have to cram them both into a single beat. This makes the sixteenth notes harder to play at high speeds.

This point is easier to understand if you experience it yourself. So try this experiment. Start playing pattern 6-7 with sixteenth notes at the start of the figures. Then gradually increase your speed. As you get faster and faster, you'll find at some point that there just isn't enough time to squeeze in both sixteenth notes before the AND of 4.

That's when you'll have to switch from pairs of sixteenth notes to eighth-note triplets as in pattern 6-6. Switching to triplets gives you an extra beat before you have to get back on the eighth-note grid – you don't have to get back until 1. Once you make the switch to triplets, you'll find you can play the pattern faster.

If you don't make the switch to triplets consciously, as your speed increases it will eventually happen automatically. You may not even realize that it's happened because at high speeds it's hard to hear the subtle difference between a pair of sixteenth notes plus an eighth note and an eighth-note triplet. If you're having a hard time hearing the difference while you play, you may want to record yourself and listen afterwards.

So here's the strategy: When a figure starts on an on-beat and you want to play it at maximum speed, use an eighth-note triplet to generate a ripple effect. When a figure starts on an offbeat and you want to play it with maximum accuracy, use a pair of sixteenth notes instead.

Okay, so far so good. But what do you do when you want to generate a ripple effect on a repeating figure that *alternates* between starting on on-beats and offbeats? That's the situation you'll face in many cross-rhythms, including the 5-beat cross- rhythm in the next chart:

PATTERN 6-8

1	+	2	+	3	+	4	+	1	+	2	+	3	+	4	+
X	X	X	X		X	X	X	X		X	X	X	X		X
X	X	X		X	X	X	X		X	X	X	X		X	X
X	X														

One strategy is to start each figure with a pair of sixteenth notes. This gives the pattern a consistent sound and makes the figures that start on offbeats easy to play. It's true that this strategy will limit your maximum overall speed slightly, but you'll still be able to generate a ripple effect. Try this strategy now, playing the figures the same way every time – RLRLR:

PATTERN 6-9

1	+	2	+	3	+	4	+	1	+	2	+	3	+	4	+
xx	X	X	X		xx	X	X	X		xx	X	X	X		xx
X	X	X		xx	X	X	X		xx	X	X	X		xx	X
X	X														

A second strategy is to alternate between triplets and sixteenth notes on each figure. Play a triplet when the figure starts on an on-beat and a pair of sixteenth notes when it starts on an offbeat. Although the figures will no longer be absolutely consistent, at high speeds most

PLAYING
PRINCIPLE

When a figure starts on an on-beat and you want to play at maximum speed, use an eighth-note triplet to generate a ripple effect.

When a figure starts on an offbeat and you want to play it with maximum accuracy, use a pair of sixteenth notes instead.

people won't be able to tell the difference. In fact, you may not even notice the difference yourself. As you approach your maximum speed, you may switch to triplets on the on-beat figures automatically, without even being aware of it.

Here's how the figures look if you alternate. Again, play each figure RLRLR:

PATTERN 6-10

1	+	2	+	3	+	4	+	1	+	2	+	3	+	4	+
x̂ x x̂	X	X			xx	X	X	X		x̂ x x̂	X	X			xx
X	X	X		x̂ x x̂	X	X			xx	X	X	X		x̂ x x̂	
X	X														

A third strategy is to start each figure with a triplet. Even though starting a triplet on an offbeat is normally hard, in this case it's not too bad. That's because every other figure – starting with the first one – starts on an on-beat.

As you play that first easy triplet, the speed will register in your hands. You just need to hold that speed in your muscle memory for a moment and then duplicate it in the next figure, which starts on an offbeat. The figure after that starts on an on-beat, so you'll be able to refresh your muscle memory all over again. By using this leap-frog process, you should be able to play triplets at the start of every figure. And remember, starting all the figures with triplets allows you to reach your maximum overall speed on the pattern:

PATTERN 6-11

1	+	2	+	3	+	4	+	1	+	2	+	3	+	4	+
x̂ x x̂	X	X		x̂ x x̂	X	X		x̂ x x̂	X	X		x̂ x			
x̂ x	X	X		x̂ x x̂	X	X		x̂ x x̂	X	X		x̂ x x̂		
X	X														

Now play the same figures, but this time alternate the voicing:

PATTERN 6-12

1	+	2	+	3	+	4	+	1	+	2	+	3	+	4	+
x x x	X	X		o o o	O	O		x x x	X	X			o o	
o o	O	O		x x x	X	X		o o o	O	O		x x x		
X	X														

Starting with an eighth-note triplet in six also takes some strategizing. Generally it's easier to start a triplet on the beats of the 6-pulse – the odd-numbered beats. When you do that, the note *following* the triplet will also fall on an odd-numbered beat. This gives you solid reference points at both the beginning and the end of the triplet.

Here are figures that start with a triplet on 1:

PATTERN 6-13

1	2	3	4	5	6	1	2	3	4	5	6
x x x	X	X				x x x	X	X			
R	L	R	L	R		R	L	R	L	R	

Here are the same figures starting on 3:

PATTERN 6-14

1	2	3	4	5	6	1	2	3	4	5	6
		x x x	X	X				x x x	X	X	
		R	L	R	L	R			R	L	R	L

And here are the same figures again starting on 5:

PATTERN 6-15

1	2	3	4	5	6	1	2	3	4	5	6
X	X			x̂ x x̂		X	X			x̂ x x̂	
L	R			R L R		L	R			R L R	

Starting a triplet on beat 2 isn't too bad either, because the note following the triplet falls on the pulse on beat 4. This gives you a solid reference point to aim for:

PATTERN 6-16

1	2	3	4	5	6	1	2	3	4	5	6
	x̂ x x̂		X	X			x̂ x x̂		X	X	
	R L R		L	R			R L R		L	R	

But starting on 4 or 6 with a triplet is harder. That's when it makes more sense to start your figures with a pair of sixteenth notes:

PATTERN 6-17

1	2	3	4	5	6	1	2	3	4	5	6
X			xx	X	X	X			xx	X	X
R			RL	R	L	R			RL	R	L

PATTERN 6-18

1	2	3	4	5	6	1	2	3	4	5	6
X	X	X			xx	X	X	X			xx
R	L	R			RL	R	L	R			RL

If you want to create a 5-beat cross-rhythm in six using figures like these, you have the same three options you had in four. You can start each figure with a pair of sixteenth notes, you can alternate between sixteenth notes and triplets, or you can rely on your muscle memory and play triplets all the way through. Here's what the cross-rhythm looks like with triplets all the way through:

PATTERN 6-19

(The grouped "x x x" notes are bracketed as eighth-note triplets.)

1	2	3	4	5	6	1	2	3	4	5	6
x	x	x	X	X		x	x	x	X	X	
X	X		x	x	x	X	X		x	x	x
	x	x	x	X	X		x	x	x	X	X
x	x	X	X		x	x	x	X	X		x
X											

Now play the same figures, but this time alternate the voicing:

PATTERN 6-20

(The grouped "x x x" and "o o o" notes are bracketed as eighth-note triplets.)

1	2	3	4	5	6	1	2	3	4	5	6
x	x	x	X	X		o	o	o	O	O	
X	X		o	o	o	O	O		x	x	x
	o	o	o	O	O		x	x	x	X	X
o	o	O	O		x	x	x	X	X		o
O											

In the lessons that follow, when we include faster strokes in figures we generally chart them as sixteenth notes. But feel free to substitute eighth-note triplets whenever you like.

Get dense and intense with four-stroke figures

Remember the *three*-stroke figures we spent so much time on back in Lesson 4? With those figures you had to make a choice. You could play them the same way every time or you could play them with pure alternating hands.

When you add a *fourth* stroke to the figures – either by starting with a pair of sixteenth notes or an eighth-note triplet – the issue evaporates. That's because the figures now have an even number of strokes:

PATTERN 7-1

1	+	2	+	3	+	4	+	1	+	2	+	3	+	4	+
xx	X	X		xx	X	X		xx	X	X		xx	X	X	
RL	R	L		RL	R	L		RL	R	L		RL	R	L	

PATTERN 7-2

1	+	2	+	3	+	4	+	1	+	2	+	3	+	4	+
x	x	x	X		x	x	x	X		x	x	x	X		x	x	x	X
R	L	R	L		R	L	R	L		R	L	R	L		R	L	R	L

Here are the same figures in six:

PATTERN 7-3

1	2	3	4	5	6	1	2	3	4	5	6
xx	X	X		xx	X	X		xx	X	X	
RL	R	L		RL	R	L		RL	R	L	

1	2	3	4	5	6	1	2	3	4	5	6
x̂	x	x	X			x̂	x	x	X		
R	L	R	L			R	L	R	L		

Now you're going to get dense and intense by playing these four-stroke figures without any empty beats between them. In six, each figure spans a single pulse. We've charted this pattern with sixteenth notes, but remember you can play it – or any other pattern we've charted with sixteenth notes – with eighth-note triplets if you like:

PATTERN 7-5

1	2	3	4	5	6	1	2	3	4	5	6
xx	X	X	xx	X	X	xx	X	X	xx	X	X
RL	R	L	RL	R	L	RL	R	L	RL	R	L

Here's the same pattern with alternating voicing:

PATTERN 7-6

1	2	3	4	5	6	1	2	3	4	5	6
xx	X	X	oo	O	O	xx	X	X	oo	O	O
RL	R	L	RL	R	L	RL	R	L	RL	R	L

Now try it with alternating pairs. Notice that you don't downshift on this pattern. You go straight from sixteenth-note slaps to eighth-note tones:

PATTERN 7-7

1	2	3	4	5	6	1	2	3	4	5	6
xx	O	O	xx	O	O	xx	O	O	xx	O	O
RL	R	L	RL	R	L	RL	R	L	RL	R	L

The next pattern is the same as pattern 7-6 except we've shifted the figures one beat to the right. Now instead of starting on a pulse, each four-stroke figure *ends* on a pulse:

PATTERN 7-8

1	2	3	4	5	6	1	2	3	4	5	6
O	xx	X	X	oo	O	O	xx	X	X	oo	O
L	RL	R	L	RL	R	L	RL	R	L	RL	R

Now we're going to show you an easy trick you can do with this pattern to bring out the elusive upbeats in six – the beats halfway between pulses. All you have to do is play just tones in the left hand and just slaps in the right. Then your left hand will be playing each pulse and upbeat – something that it would have a hard time doing any other way. To hear the polyrhythm, you've got to play this pattern along with a timeline or a song in six:

PATTERN 7-9

1	2	3	4	5	6	1	2	3	4	5	6
O	xo	X	O	xo	X	O	xo	X	O	xo	X
L	RL	R	L	RL	R	L	RL	R	L	RL	R

Now let's get dense and intense in four. When you take out the empty beats between the four-stroke figures in pattern 7-1, you get a 3-beat cross-rhythm. In the next pattern, this cross-rhythm runs until the middle of the second measure. We've added an extra slap at the end so you can end on a pulse:

PATTERN 7-10

1	+	2	+	3	+	4	+	1	+	2	+	3	+	4	+
xx	X	X	xx	X	X	xx	X	X	xx	X	X	X			
RL	R	L	RL	R	L	RL	R	L	RL	R	L	R			

In the next chart, we've extended the pattern so it ends on ONE:

PATTERN 7-11

1	+	2	+	3	+	4	+	1	+	2	+	3	+	4	+
xx	X	X	xx	X	X	xx	X	X	xx	X	X	xx	X	X	X
RL	R	L	RL	R	L	RL	R	L	RL	R	L	RL	R	L	R
X															
L															

Now play the same pattern with alternating voicing:

PATTERN 7-12

1	+	2	+	3	+	4	+	1	+	2	+	3	+	4	+
xx	X	X	oo	O	O	xx	X	X	oo	O	O	xx	X	X	X
RL	R	L	RL	R	L	RL	R	L	RL	R	L	RL	R	L	R
X															
L															

One way to heighten the effect of the dense pattern you just played is by setting it up first with a more spacious pattern. That's what we've done in the next chart. In the first cycle, you start with the same figures, but with empty beats between them. This introduces the theme of the pattern and creates a context for the dense cycle that follows. The contrast between the spacious first cycle and dense second cycle adds momentum to the pattern and builds excitement. Notice we've added empty rows to the chart to make it easier to read:

PATTERN 7-13

1	+	2	+	3	+	4	+	1	+	2	+	3	+	4	+
xx	X	X		oo	O	O		xx	X	X		oo	O	O	
RL	R	L		RL	R	L		RL	R	L		RL	R	L	
xx	X	X	oo	O	O	xx	X	X	oo	O	O	xx	X	X	X
RL	R	L	RL	R	L	RL	R	L	RL	R	L	RL	R	L	R
X															
L															

Now let's supersize the last pattern by doubling everything. Start by playing two cycles of the spacious pattern and then play two cycles of the dense cross-rhythm (again we've added empty rows to make the chart easier to read):

1	+	2	+	3	+	4	+	1	+	2	+	3	+	4	+
xx	X	X		oo	O	O		xx	X	X		oo	O	O	
RL	R	L		RL	R	L		RL	R	L		RL	R	L	
xx	X	X		oo	O	O		xx	X	X		oo	O	O	
RL	R	L		RL	R	L		RL	R	L		RL	R	L	
xx	X	X	oo	O	O	xx	X	X	oo	O	O	xx	X	X	oo
RL	R	L	RL	R	L	RL	R	L	RL	R	L	RL	R	L	RL
O	O	xx	X	X	oo	O	O	xx	X	X	oo	O	O	xx	X
R	L	RL	R	L	RL	R	L	RL	R	L	RL	R	L	RL	R
X															
L															

Lead with your strong hand on faster strokes

Leading with your strong hand on faster strokes is another strategy that flows from an acceptance of our handedness. It's not that your weak hand is necessarily slower than your strong hand. It's just that it doesn't like to go first. In fact, your weak hand would rather take the lead at the start of a pattern if it means it can get out of leading on faster strokes later on. So your first priority should be to lead with your strong hand on faster strokes. Everything else you do should be arranged around it.

The figures in the first pattern start with an eighth-note slap followed by a pair of sixteenth-note tones. In order to lead with your right hand on the faster strokes, you need to start each figure with your left. Notice that after you've played the tones, you need to lead with your left hand again when the voicing changes to slaps. Take your time getting to know these figures because we'll be working with them for most of this lesson:

PATTERN 8-1

1	2	3	4	5	6	1	2	3	4	5	6
	X	oo	O	X	X		X	oo	O	X	X
	L	RL	R	L	R		L	RL	R	L	R

Now combine one of these figures with two strokes on even-numbered beats:

PATTERN 8-2

1	2	3	4	5	6	1	2	3	4	5	6
	X	oo	O	X	X		X		X		
	L	RL	R	L	R		L		R		

If you start the figure over again on 6 in the second measure, the repeating figure creates a 10-beat cross-rhythm:

PATTERN 8-3

1	2	3	4	5	6	1	2	3	4	5	6
	X	oo	O	X	X		X		X		X
	L	RL	R	L	R		L		R		L
oo	O	X	X		X		X		X		
RL	R	L	R		L		R		L		

Here's the same figure you started with, only this time you'll play it twice in four:

PATTERN 8-4

1	+	2	+	3	+	4	+	1	+	2	+	3	+	4	+
	X	oo	O	X	X			X	oo	O	X	X			
	L	RL	R	L	R			L	RL	R	L	R			

If you keep going, you end up with a 6-beat cross-rhythm. Here's the complete cycle of that cross-rhythm:

PATTERN 8-5

1	+	2	+	3	+	4	+	1	+	2	+	3	+	4	+
	X	oo	O	X	X		X	oo	O	X	X		X	oo	O
X	X		X	oo	O	X	X		X	oo	O	X	X		X
oo	O	X	X		X	oo	O	X	X		X	oo	O	X	X

In the next pattern, you'll play the figure twice and then round things out with a couple of offbeats. Notice you start on the AND of 4 in the second measure:

PATTERN 8-6

1	+	2	+	3	+	4	+	1	+	2	+	3	+	4	+
oo	O	X	X		X	oo	O	X	X		X		X		<u>X</u>
RL	R	L	R		L	RL	R	L	R		L		R		L

Now put it all together to create a short solo:

PATTERN 8-7

1	+	2	+	3	+	4	+	1	+	2	+	3	+	4	+
															X
															L
oo	O	X	X		X	oo	O	X	X		X		X		X
RL	R	L	R		L	RL	R	L	R		L		R		L
oo	O	X	X		X	oo	O	X	X		X		X		X
RL	R	L	R		L	RL	R	L	R		L		R		L
oo	O	X	X		X	oo	O	X	X		X	oo	O	X	X
RL	R	L	R		L	RL	R	L	R		L	RL	R	L	R
	X	oo	O	X	X		X	oo	O	X	X		X	oo	O
	L	RL	R	L	R		L	RL	R	L	R		L	RL	R
X	X		X		X	X		X	X	X					
L	R		L		R	L		R	L	L					

Now let's go back to six and play a continuous pattern that alternates in three's – three slaps followed by three tones. If you start with your left hand, you'll be all set up to lead with your right on the sixteenth notes:

PATTERN 8-8

1	2	3	4	5	6	1	2	3	4	5	6
X	X	X	oo	O	X	X	X	oo	O	X	X
L	R	L	RL	R	L	R	L	RL	R	L	R
X											
L											

If you found it hard to lead with your left hand on the slaps in this pattern, you may want to start by practicing threes with just eighth notes at first:

PATTERN 8-9

1	2	3	4	5	6	1	2	3	4	5	6
X	X	X	O	O	O	X	X	X	O	O	O
L	R	L	R	L	R	L	R	L	R	L	R

The next pattern is the same as pattern 8-8 except that you start with a four-stroke group of slaps before switching to threes:

PATTERN 8-10

1	2	3	4	5	6	1	2	3	4	5	6
xx	X	X	oo	O	X	X	X	oo	O	X	X
X											

Now let's combine variations of these patterns to create a short solo:

PATTERN 8-11

1	2	3	4	5	6	1	2	3	4	5	6
xx	X	X	oo	O	X	X	X		X		X
RL	R	L	RL	R	L	R	L		R		L
xx	X	X	oo	O	X	X	X		X		X
RL	R	L	RL	R	L	R	L		R		L
xx	X	X	oo	O	O	xx	X	X	oo	O	O
RL	R	L	RL	R	L	RL	R	L	RL	R	L
xx	X	X	oo	O	O	xx	X	X	oo	O	O
RL	R	L	RL	R	L	RL	R	L	RL	R	L
xx	X	X	oo	O	X	X	X	oo	O	X	X
RL	R	L	RL	R	L	R	L	RL	R	L	R
X	oo	O	X	X	X	oo	O	X	X	X	oo
L	RL	R	L	R	L	RL	R	L	R	L	RL
O	X	X	X	oo	O	X	X	X	oo	O	X
R	L	R	L	RL	R	L	R	L	RL	R	L
X		X	X								
R		L	R								

Here are the same alternating threes in four:

PATTERN 8-12

1	+	2	+	3	+	4	+	1	+	2	+	3	+	4	+
X	X	X	oo	O	X	X	X	oo	O	X	X	X	oo	O	X
X	X														

The next pattern starts with the original figure. In the second cycle, we've taken out the empty beats between the original figures to create a continuous pattern of alternating threes:

PATTERN 8-13

1	+	2	+	3	+	4	+	1	+	2	+	3	+	4	+
	X	oo	O	X	X		X	oo	O	X	X		X	oo	O
X	X	X	oo	O	X	X	X	oo	O	X	X	X	oo	O	X
X	X														

Although leading with your strong hand on faster strokes is the easiest way to play them, there will be times when you won't be able to follow this strategy. For example, if you want to create a continuous pattern with an odd figure that starts with faster strokes, you'll have to lead with your weak hand on every other repetition:

PATTERN 8-14

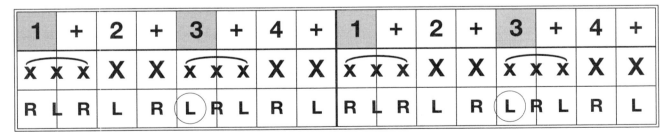

Leave space around a flam

A **flam** is a double stroke in which both hands play with equal force almost simultaneously. One hand plays *just before* the beat and the other *directly on* the beat. The two strokes can be the same – two slaps or two tones – or different – a bass and a slap or a slap and a tone. In this lesson we'll be focusing on the most common flam, a flam made with two slaps. But feel free to experiment with other combinations.

Flams can be used just like a pair of sixteenth notes to create a ripple effect. All you need to do is follow them with slower strokes in the same voice. Here's a pattern with sixteenth notes that you played earlier:

PATTERN 7-5

1	2	3	4	5	6	1	2	3	4	5	6
xx	X	X	xx	X	X	xx	X	X	xx	X	X
RL	R	L	RL	R	L	RL	R	L	RL	R	L

PLAYING PRINCIPLE

Leading with your strong hand on flams allows you to freely substitute them for sixteenth notes.

Now replace the sixteenth notes with flams. Notice that the hand pattern stays the same. Leading with your strong hand on flams allows you to freely substitute them for sixteenth notes in patterns like these:

PATTERN 9-1

1	2	3	4	5	6	1	2	3	4	5	6
ˣX	X	X	ˣX	X	X	ˣX	X	X	ˣX	X	X
RL	R	L	RL	R	L	RL	R	L	RL	R	L

You may have found this pattern a little harder to play with flams than with sixteenth notes. That's because the timing of the first stroke is trickier with the flam. With the pair of sixteenth notes, you get to play the first stroke right on the beat. With the flam, you have to play the first stroke just before the beat.

Because the timing and coordination on a flam are both tricky, it's nice to have a moment to collect yourself before and after launching one. The way to do this is to leave at least one empty beat on both sides of a flam. Leaving space around a flam also helps make it stand out when you want to create a dramatic effect.

The next pattern is a common djembe break that ends with a flam. Notice that you get two full beats to collect yourself before you have to play it and plenty of time after to prepare for whatever's next. Because the flam comes at the end of the phrase, it functions like an exclamation point at the end of a sentence. And because it's played in a different voice, it stands out even more:

PATTERN 9-2

1	2	3	4	5	6	1	2	3	4	5	6
oo	O	O	O	O		O	O		O		
RL	R	L	R	L		R	L		R		
ˣX											
RL											

The next pattern is another common djembe break. This time the flam comes at the beginning of the phrase, where it functions as an attention grabber. Again space and voicing make it stand out:

PATTERN 9-3

1	+	2	+	3	+	4	+	1	+	2	+	3	+	4	+
ˣX		O	O		O			O	O		O		O		
RL		R	L		R			L	R		L		R		

You can also use a flam to turn an odd figure into an even one by replacing a single eighth note with the two strokes of the flam. This

Make an odd figure
even by replacing
an isolated single
stroke with a flam.

will allow you to repeat the figure without having to break the flow of alternating hands.

The best candidates for flamming are isolated single strokes, like the slaps in pattern 4-19. Play the original pattern first to refresh your memory:

PATTERN 4-19

1	+	2	+	3	+	4	+	1	+	2	+	3	+	4	+
	O	O		O	O		X		O	O		O	O		X
	R	L		R	L		R		R	L		R	L		R

Replacing each single slap with a flam allows you to repeat the figure without breaking the flow of alternating hands. It also thickens the texture and pumps up the volume on the AND of 4:

PATTERN 9-4

1	+	2	+	3	+	4	+	1	+	2	+	3	+	4	+
	O	O		O	O		ˣX		O	O		O	O		ˣX
	R	L		R	L		RL		R	L		R	L		RL

The isolated slap on 3 in the following version of the 6/8 bell is another likely candidate for flamming. Try it first without the flam:

PATTERN 4-18

1	2	3	4	5	6	1	2	3	4	5	6
O		X		O̲	O		O		O		O
L		R		R	L		R		L		R

Replacing the isolated slap with a flam turns this seven-stroke figure into an eight-stroke figure:

1	2	3	4	5	6	1	2	3	4	5	6
O		^{x}X		O	O		O		O		O
L		R		R	L		R		L		R

The next pattern is based on the three-stroke broken figure from pattern 4-22. Replacing the single slap with a flam creates a dramatic four-stroke figure with a high flam-to-stroke ratio:

PATTERN 9-6

1	+	2	+	3	+	4	+	1	+	2	+	3	+	4	+
^{x}X		O	O												
RL		R	L												
^{x}X		O	O												
RL		R	L												
^{x}X		O	O	^{x}X		O	O	^{x}X		O	O				
RL		R	L	RL		R	L	RL		R	L				
^{x}X		O	O												
RL		R	L												

In the next pattern we've used the same figure again to create a 6-beat cross-rhythm that ends with a flam on ONE. Even though there's a two-beat rest between figures, that shouldn't be a problem because each figure starts on an on-beat:

1	+	2	+	3	+	4	+	1	+	2	+	3	+	4	+
	ˣX			O	O			ˣX		O	O			ˣX	
O	O			ˣX		O	O		ˣX			O	O		
ˣX															

The last pattern in this lesson comes from a support drum part in the Ghanaian rhythm agbazja. In the second cycle you have to play four flams in a row. But because there's space around each one you should have plenty of time to regroup:

PATTERN 9-8

1	2	3	4	5	6	1	2	3	4	5	6
	ˣX		O	O	O		ˣX		O	O	O
	RL		R	L	R		RL		R	L	R
	ˣX		ˣX		ˣX		ˣX		O	O	O
	RL		RL		RL		RL		R	L	R

Use the compression trick to create complex cross-rhythms the easy way

Compression can refer to taking out empty beats between figures or taking out empty beats within figures. It can also refer to playing strokes closer together, such as squeezing two strokes into the space of one by converting two eighth notes into sixteenth notes. That's the kind of compression you'll be doing in this lesson.

To do the specific form of compression we call the **compression trick**, you need to start with a sequence of continuous eighth notes consisting of alternating groups of slaps and tones. It's easiest if each group has an even number of strokes: 4 slaps and 4 tones, 2 slaps and 4 tones, 4 slaps and 6 tones, etc. Then all you do is compress the first two tones in each group by playing them twice as fast, converting them from eighth notes to sixteenth notes. The result is a continuous cross-rhythm that sounds hard but is easy to play.

The easiest sequence to do the compression trick on is a sequence of alternating fours – four slaps and four tones. So that's the sequence we'll be using as our starting point. Here's the sequence in four with eighth notes:

PATTERN 10-1

1	+	2	+	3	+	4	+	1	+	2	+	3	+	4	+
X	X	X	X	O	O	O	O	X	X	X	X	O	O	O	O
R	L	R	L	R	L	R	L	R	L	R	L	R	L	R	L

By compressing the first two tones in each group of four you can turn this square pattern into a dynamic 7-beat cross-rhythm with a built-in ripple effect:

8-BEAT ORIGINAL PATTERN

1	+	2	+	3	+	4	+
X	X	X	X	O	O	O	O
R	L	R	L	R	L	R	L

7-BEAT PATTERN AFTER COMPRESSION TRICK

1	+	2	+	3	+	4
X	X	X	X	oo	O	O
R	L	R	L	RL	R	L

Notice that although the compressed pattern only has a 7-beat cycle, you still play the same eight strokes. This means that all the easy strategies built into the original pattern carry over into the compressed version: You still lead with your strong hand at the start of the pattern and on changes in voicing. And you still alternate hands all the way through.

The only thing that's different in the compressed pattern is that you've introduced sixteenth notes. But you do that in a way that follows the easy strategies you've learned for adding faster strokes: You lead with your strong hand, you use only a single pair of sixteenth notes, and you downshift to maximize the ripple effect.

Now you can begin to see why the compression trick works so well. It incorporates almost all the hand-pattern strategies you've learned so far. When you apply it to alternating fours the result is the easiest 7-beat cross-rhythm you'll ever play. You'll hardly have to think about your hands at all, so your mind will be free to focus on tracking the pulse and keeping your place in the rhythm.

Now play three and a half repetitions of the compressed sequence:

PATTERN 10-2

1	+	2	+	3	+	4	+	1	+	2	+	3	+	4	+
X	X	X	X	oo	O	O	X	X	X	X	oo	O	O	X	X
R	L	R	L	RL	R	L	R	L	R	L	RL	R	L	R	L
X	X	oo	O	O	X	X	X	X							
R	L	RL	R	L	R	L	R	L							

See how easy it is? We cut this pattern off, but you can play the sequence indefinitely if you want. As a matter of fact, you may want to light some candles, burn some incense, and have at it.

Once you get comfortable with this sequence, you can tack a section of it onto almost any other pattern. Ending with a burst of compressed alternating fours is a great way to finish a phrase with a flourish. All you need to do is find a natural place to overlap with the original pattern to create a seamless transition.

Ending with a burst of compressed alternating fours is a great way to finish a phrase with a flourish.

In the next pattern, we've done just that. We start with a phrase based on variations of a three-stroke figure. Then in the fifth cycle we've tacked on some compressed alternating fours. Notice that the start of the compressed pattern overlaps with three slaps from the original phrase to create a smooth transition (we've bracketed the overlap). The effect is like shifting into overdrive:

1	+	2	+	3	+	4	+	1	+	2	+	3	+	4	+
													O	O	X
													R	L	R
	X	X	X		O	O	X						O	O	X
	R	L	R		R	L	R						R	L	R
	X	X	X		O	O	X						O	O	X
	R	L	R		R	L	R						R	L	R
	X	X	X		O	O	X		X	X	X		O	O	X
	R	L	R		R	L	R		R	L	R		R	L	R
	[X	X	X]	X	oo	O	O	X	X	X	X	oo	O	O	X
	R	L	R	L	RL	R	L	R	L	R	L	RL	R	L	R
X	X	X	oo	O	O	X	X	X	X	oo	O	O	X	X	X
L	R	L	RL	R	L	R	L	R	L	RL	R	L	R	L	R
X															
L															

Here's what compressed alternating fours look like in six:

PATTERN 10-4

1	2	3	4	5	6	1	2	3	4	5	6
X	X	X	X	oo	O	O	X	X	X	X	oo
R	L	R	L	RL	R	L	R	L	R	L	RL
O	O	X	X	X	X	oo	O	O	X	X	X
R	L	R	L	R	L	RL	R	L	R	L	R
X											
L											

Now let's tack a section of this 7-beat cross-rhythm onto a figure you played back in Lesson 6. Again we've created a smooth transition by finding a natural place to overlap with the original figure:

PATTERN 10-5

1	2	3	4	5	6	1	2	3	4	5	6
											oo
											RL
O	O	X	X		oo	O	O	X	X		oo
R	L	R	L		RL	R	L	R	L		RL
O	O	X	X	X	X	oo	O	O	X	X	X
R	L	R	L	R	L	RL	R	L	R	L	R
X											
L											

Next let's try the compression trick on a sequence consisting of continuous alternating *twos* and fours – two slaps and four tones. Here's that sequence in six with eighth notes:

PATTERN 10-6

1	2	3	4	5	6	1	2	3	4	5	6
X	X	O	O	O	O	X	X	O	O	O	O
R	L	R	L	R	L	R	L	R	L	R	L

Here's what the compressed version looks like. Notice that the six-stroke sequence now creates a 5-beat cross-rhythm:

PATTERN 10-7

1	2	3	4	5	6	1	2	3	4	5	6
X	X	oo	O	O	X	X	oo	O	O	X	X
R	L	RL	R	L	R	L	RL	R	L	R	L
oo	O	O	X	X	oo	O	O	X	X		
RL	R	L	R	L	RL	R	L	R	L		

Now let's put this 5-beat cross-rhythm in context by using it in a short solo. We start with alternating pairs and gradually increase the density with figures that foreshadow the cross-rhythm. Then we use the full cross-rhythm to build to a climax:

1	2	3	4	5	6	1	2	3	4	5	6
	O	O		X	X		O	O		X	X
	R	L		R	L		R	L		R	L
	O	O		X	X		O	O		X	X
	R	L		R	L		R	L		R	L
oo	O	O		X	X		O	O		X	X
RL	R	L		R	L		R	L		R	L
oo	O	O		X	X		O	O		X	X
RL	R	L		R	L		R	L		R	L
oo	O	O		X	X	oo	O	O		X	X
RL	R	L		R	L	RL	R	L		R	L
oo	O	O	X	X	oo	O	O	X	X	oo	O
RL	R	L	R	L	RL	R	L	R	L	RL	R
O	X	X	oo	O	O	X	X	oo	O	O	X
L	R	L	RL	R	L	R	L	RL	R	L	R
X											
L											

By the way, this isn't the first time you've used the compression trick to create a continuous 5-beat cross-rhythm. You did it back in Lesson 8 in patterns like this one:

PATTERN 8-8

1	2	3	4	5	6	1	2	3	4	5	6
X	X	X	oo	O	X	X	X	oo	O	X	X
L	R	L	RL	R	L	R	L	RL	R	L	R
X											
L											

Although we didn't talk about the compression trick back then, you can see now that that's what was going on. This pattern is simply a compressed sequence of alternating threes.

You probably found the 5-beat cross-rhythm in pattern 8-8 a little harder to play than the one you played in pattern 10-8. That's because pattern 8-8 has an *odd* number of strokes in each group, which means you have to lead with your weak hand every time you switch to slaps. You also have to play a pattern that alternates in threes with hands that alternate in twos. But with practice and a reasonably good left hand, you should be able play alternating threes almost as fast as alternating fours.

Now let's move on and apply the compression trick to another sequence consisting of groups with an even number of strokes. The new sequence alternates between fours and *sixes* – four slaps and *six* tones.

In the next chart we've gone straight to the compressed pattern. Notice that it creates a 9-beat cross-rhythm which fits evenly within a span of three pulses in six. This even fit makes the pattern easy to play because each repetition starts on a pulse. We've cut the last repetition short because we wanted to end the pattern on a pulse too:

PATTERN 10-9

1	2	3	4	5	6	1	2	3	4	5	6
X	X	X	X	oo	O	O	O	O	X	X	X
R	L	R	L	RL	R	L	R	L	R	L	R
X	oo	O	O	O	O	X	X	X	X		
L	RL	R	L	R	L	R	L	R	L		

Here's a short example of how the compressed four-six sequence looks in four:

PATTERN 10-10

1	+	2	+	3	+	4	+	1	+	2	+	3	+	4	+
X	X	X	X	oo	O	O	O	O	X	X	X				
R	L	R	L	RL	R	L	R	L	R	L	R				

Now we're going to add another level of complexity by transferring this compressed four-six sequence onto the quarter-note triplet grid in four. Whew, that was a mouthful! But don't worry, it's not as hard as it sounds. When you get to the first two tones, just keep feeling the triplets and double the speed of your hands:

PATTERN 10-11

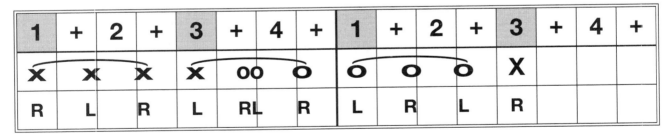

1	+	2	+	3	+	4	+	1	+	2	+	3	+	4	+
x	x	x	x	oo	O	O	O	O	X						
R	L	R	L	RL	R	L	R	L	R						

Once you're comfortable playing this compressed sequence on the quarter-note triplet grid, try extending the pattern so you can end on ONE:

PATTERN 10-12

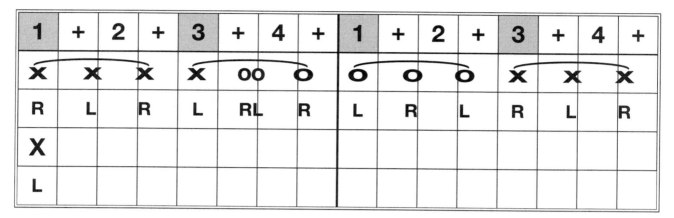

Now extend the pattern even further, so it ends on the last pulse in the second cycle:

PATTERN 10-13

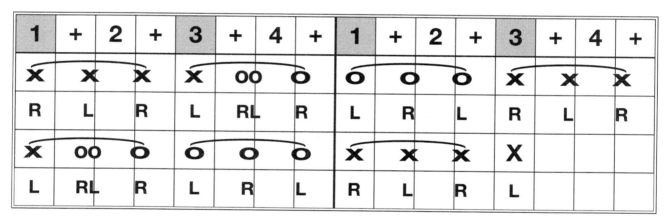

The next pattern is nothing more than the bottom row of the pattern you just played. We've isolated it because we're going to modify it in the pattern that follows. Notice you start with your left hand:

PATTERN 10-14

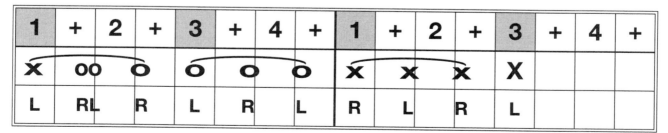

The next pattern is the same as the one you just played except we've taken out the slap on ONE. Leaving off the first note of a triplet is a nice way to ease into a pattern. It's like taking a breath before diving into a pool. You just have to make sure that you still *feel* the pulse on ONE as part of the first triplet even though you're not playing it. Notice that the remaining sequence is six-four instead of four-six – you start with tones instead of slaps:

Leave off the first note of a quarter-note triplet.

PATTERN 10-15

1	+	2	+	3	+	4	+	1	+	2	+	3	+	4	+
−	oo	o	o	o	o	x	x	x	X						
RL	R	L	R	L	R	L	R	L							

In the next chart we've extended the pattern by repeating the six-four sequence twice:

PATTERN 10-16

1	+	2	+	3	+	4	+	1	+	2	+	3	+	4	+
−	oo	o	o	o	o	x	x	x	x	oo	o				
	RL	R	L	R	L	R	L	R	L	RL	R				
o	o	o	x	x	x	X									
L	R	L	R	L	R	L									

Now combine variations to create a longer phrase:

PATTERN 10-17

1	+	2	+	3	+	4	+	1	+	2	+	3	+	4	+
–	oo	o͡	o͡	o	o	x͡	x	x͡	X						
	RL	R	L	R	L	R	L	R	L						
–	oo	o͡	o͡	o	o	x͡	x	x͡	X						
	RL	R	L	R	L	R	L	R	L						
–	oo	o͡	o͡	o	o	x͡	x	x͡	x	oo	o				
	RL	R	L	R	L	R	L	R	L	RL	R				
o	o	o͡	x͡	x	x͡	X									
L	R	L	R	L	R	L									

Now that you understand the compression trick, you should be able to use it on other sequences of alternating slaps and tones. You can also combine different sequences in a single pattern. For example, you can start with alternating fours and then shift into an alternating four-six sequence. The possibilities are endless. Play around and see what you come up with. Just remember the trick is easiest to do when you use an even number of slaps and an even number of tones.

The possibilities are endless.

Glossary

alternating pairs: two slaps followed by two tones or vice versa.

broken figure: a figure with empty beats in it.

camouflaging: the use of voicing to disguise the structure of a pattern.

compression : taking out empty beats between figures, taking out empty beats within figures, or playing strokes closer together.

compression trick: compressing the first two tones in a continuous sequence of strokes consisting of alternating groups of slaps and tones.

continuous figure: a figures without empty beats in it.

cycle of a figure: the number of beats from the start of one repetition of a figure to the start of the next.

downshifting: moving from faster to slower strokes while staying in the same voice.

even figure: a figure with an even number of strokes.

odd figure: a figure with an odd number of strokes.

on-off style: a style of playing where your strong hand plays all the strokes that fall on the on-beats and your weak hand plays all the strokes that fall on the offbeats.

pure alternating hands: continuing the flow of alternating hands from figure to figure even though it reverses the hand pattern on every repetition.

repeating figure: a figure that stays exactly the same on every repetition, keeping the same structure and the same voicing.

ripple effect: the lingering impression of speed when faster strokes are immediately followed by slower strokes.

say-it-and-play-it: a method of learning a pattern by vocalizing it while tapping the pulse.

Also available from Dancing Hands Music

$24.95

Conga Drumming
A Beginner's Guide to Playing with Time

BY ALAN DWORSKY AND BETSY SANSBY

This 160-page book with CD is a complete, step-by-step course on conga drumming. It teaches families of drum parts for several authentic Afro-Caribbean rhythms, including rumba, bomba, calypso, conga, and bembe. We use a simple charting system and the same friendly teaching style as in SECRETS OF THE HAND. Life-like illustrations show you the proper technique for each stroke. And the CD that's included contains a sample recording of each of the 175 drum parts taught in the book as well examples of how the parts sound together.

DRUM MAGAZINE
Best Percussion Method Book
2000 READERS' POLL

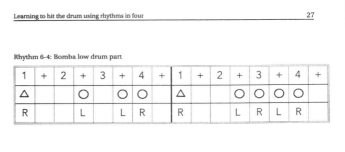

Learning to hit the drum using rhythms in four   27

Rhythm 6-4: Bomba low drum part

1	+	2	+	3	+	4	+	1	+	2	+	3	+	4	+
△				O		O	O	△				O	O	O	O
R				L		L	R	R				L	R	L	R

To make the slap, start from the same position that you started from to make the open tone. Pivot your hand upward from the wrist. Then whip your fingers down onto the drumhead while driving your palm down and slightly forward onto the edge of the drum. Cup your hand so that only the pads of the fingertips hit the head. The cup should be slight; you should only be able to slide a pencil between your palm and the drumhead, not a golf ball.

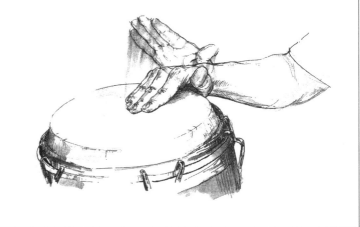

$29.95

Featuring instruction by renowned percussionist **Jorge Bermudez**

Conga Drumming
A Beginner's Video Guide

This video gives you a chance to see how all the basic patterns from the CONGA DRUMMING book are supposed to be played. And it's a great way to learn proper playing technique, because we teach each stroke using multiple camera angles and slow-motion photography.

"A <u>must-see</u> for all beginners."
– MICKEY HART

With sizzling solos on congas and bongos by special guest **Raul Rekow** of **Santana**

and electrifying performances by Cuban dancer **Rosie Lopez Moré**, from the legendary Tropicana nightclub in Havana.

"Few videos capture the spirit of fun as well as CONGA DRUMMING. All the basics are covered and the educational information is interspersed with burning performances by the ensemble. When Rosie Lopez Moré is on screen the video is ablaze with energy."
– DRUM MAGAZINE

"Slammin! The best video for learning to play congas."
– CHALO EDUARDO, PERCUSSIONIST WITH SERGIO MENDES

Hip Grooves for Hand Drums
How to play funk, rock & world-beat patterns on any drum

BY ALAN DWORSKY AND BETSY SANSBY

This is the book for hand drummers who want to play contemporary music. It's filled with great dance grooves, many of them adapted from drumset patterns used in rock, pop, and funk music. You can play these grooves on any hand drum – a djembe, a conga, or any drum where you can get both hands on the head. The CD that comes with the book has samples of all the patterns and extended tracks so you can play along. Whether you want to play in a band, jam in the park, or just drum along with your favorite CDs, this book will show you how, step by step.

$24.95

World-Beat & Funk Grooves
Playing a Drumset the Easy Way

BY ALAN DWORSKY AND BETSY SANSBY

"It doesn't get any more accessible than this"
– DRUM MAGAZINE

This book takes African, Afro-Cuban, and funk grooves and applies them to the drumset in a linear style. It uses an ingenious method that makes complex rhythms magically emerge out of simple sequences of body movements. Within days you'll be playing patterns that usually take months to master. It comes with 2 CDs: one contains samples of every pattern in the book, the other is a timelines CD you can play along with while you practice.

$24.95

Free sample lesson at dancinghands.com

Jaguar at Half Moon Lake

BY DANCING HANDS

"A luminous debut." – NEW MUSIC SERIES REVIEW

This CD of original music features Indie-award winning Dean Magraw on acoustic guitar and several world percussionists, including master drummer Coster Massamba on djembe.

$13.95